STUNT FLYING
IN THE
MOVIES

No. 2304
$21.95

STUNT FLYING
IN THE
MOVIES

BY JIM & MAXINE GREENWOOD

TAB BOOKS Inc.

BLUE RIDGE SUMMIT, PA. 17214

Other TAB books by the author:

No. 2224   *Parachuting for Sport—2nd Edition*

FIRST EDITION

FIRST PRINTING

Copyright © 1982 by James R. Greenwood

Printed in the United States of America

Library of Congress Cataloging in Publication Data

Greenwood, Jim.
    Stunt flying in the movies.

    Bibliography: p.
    Includes index.
    1. Stunt flying. I. Greenwood, Maxine, II. Title.
TL711.S8G73   797.5′5′0973   81-18281
ISBN 0-8306-0304-2   AACR2

CONTENTS

Foreword

There had to be a link between the fantasy of the film and the pragmatic realism of aviation—a link that forged a natural partnership.

Jim Greenwood, consummate professional and incurable bird-lover, and his wife Maxine, have found that link: the gallant stunt pilots who for years have labored unsung to bring flying thrills onto theater screens and television sets. Unsung, that is, until the Greenwoods decided to write this long-awaited and badly needed book.

Herein both movie fans and airplane buffs will discover a plethora of enjoyment—the full behind-the-scenes story of a marriage literally made in heaven: the motion picture and the airplane. It's all here, from the fascinating account of the making of *Wings*, the first great aviation movie, to the brilliantly conceived large screen flying films produced for the magnificent National Air and Space Museum. More important, however, it is a tale of personalities—the Dick Graces, Frank Clarkes, Ormer Locklears, Paul Mantzs, and all the others whose bravery and bravado put audiences into countless cockpits and flight decks. Plus much more . . . .

Did Howard Hughes really buy a full-size German zeppelin for his memorable *Hell's Angels?* How was that hair-raising 747-Beechcraft collision in *Airport '75* filmed? What famed movie star got his start in a two-minute bit role in *Wings*? The answers are all in this scrupulously researched, crisply written book; it is history, nostalgia, humor, and excitement all in one volume—a bell-ringing, bugle-blowing tribute to courage, dedication, and ingenuity.

Aviation occasionally has suffered at the hands of movie makers. Every pilot I know has simultaneously winced and cursed at some of the technical errors and raw bloopers that too often afflict airplane scenes—most frequently, I fear, in careless made-for-television films. A script calls for a brief stock shot of a jetliner landing in Los Angeles supposedly after a nonstop flight from New York—except that the aircraft shown is a 727 which doesn't have transcontinental range. Or a shot of a 707 in flight, cutting to the interior—which is that of a DC-8. We see a 707 make an emergency landing and the passengers evacuate quickly down escape chutes—great scene, until a close look reveals that the cameras are filming a DC-7's chutes. I remember one TV movie in which a teenager ditches a 707 in a stormy sea with all flaps up.

Yet for every such boo-boo there have

been compensating moments of movie-making genius. Like the explosive decompression scene in *Airport*—a setup supervised by Lockheed technicians, and so complex that the first take had to be perfect because re-shooting it would have cost a fortune. The Greenwoods give us both the sublime and the ridiculous in their account—the highs and the lows, as it were, in aviation films. But that was what I expected from Jim Greenwood: I've known him for years and among his finer attributes are a sense of fairness, objectivity, and belief in factual veracity.

Having read the manuscript, I wish for two things. First, that my late brother Rod had lived to read it also. Rod had a personal experience with one of the legendary stunt pilots who populate the Greenwoods' book: the late, great Frank Tallman, who flew a Nieuport fighter in a *Twilight Zone* episode. It was a memorable script in which a World War I pursuit pilot flies into a mysterious cloud to escape German Fokkers and emerges from the cloud to find himself landing at a Strategic Air Command Base in the 1960s. The "SAC base" used for the filming was Edwards, and Rod loved to tell me about watching Tallman land the old Nieuport amid a cluster of Globemasters, B-52s and other assorted military jets, and the half-amused, half-awed faces of the modern airmen witnessing the scene. I suspect that somewhere in the Twilight Zone inhabited by the Rod Serlings and Frank Tallmans, those two bird-lovers have done some heavy reminiscing.

My second wish is purely selfish. Namely, that I had written this book myself.

Robert J. Serling
Tucson, Arizona

Introduction

Some years ago several aviation writers were whooping it up in a corner of Vince Barnett's popular Santa Monica bistro, once a favorite watering hole for pilots, assorted film folk, and a fair sprinkling of Los Angeles area night people. Vince, a veteran pilot himself (he flew the airmail in the 1920s) and a longtime film comic and character actor, suddenly halted the noisy conversation and growled: "Why don't you bums write more stories about the poor guys who fly all that junk for the movies—they bust their butts and never even get a credit line!"

Our host (who died in 1977) had a point. Here we were preaching to the choir again. We were yakking away about the men and machines (and the ladies, too) who had created and performed some of the greatest air stunts in Hollywood history. Yet with few notable exceptions, the pilots who crash planes, fly through storms, and dogfight in the sky for motion pictures are little known outside the aviation community.

Frank Clarke, Dick Grace, Paul Mantz. Sure, the flying buffs may recognize the names; but the general public probably never heard of them (Mantz being a possible exception). Most theatergoers only relate the stars to the planes they appear to be flying in aviation films.

The real aces of the silver screen, however, are the skilled guys and gals who actually fly those incredibly spectacular aerial sequences while the make-believe heroes sit it out comfortably and safely and securely on the ground.

That's not to say there are *no* pilots in the producing, directing, writing, or acting end of the motion picture business. There have been many—and there still are. Jimmy Stewart's a pilot; he flew in World War II. John Monk Saunders and William Wellman, writer and director respectively of the film *Wings*, which won the first Academy Award as the "best picture" of 1927-28, were both pilots in World War I. Cecil B. DeMille, an industry giant, learned to fly in 1917 and subsequently operated an air service. Screen star Wallace Beery also piloted his own airplane.

Among today's movie colonists who fly, Cliff Robertson is one of the most active. He owns a whole fleet of planes. As a young boy George Roy Hill, who produced and directed *The Great Waldo Pepper*, used to watch the likes of Dick Grace and Frank Clarke; he now enjoys flying his own open cockpit Waco biplane to widely scattered movie locations. George Kennedy got interested in flying while playing "Joe Patroni" in the *Airport* movies and now operates his own plane for personal transportation. Actor Gene Raymond, a longtime pilot, is jet-rated.

There have been a number of fine magazine articles on the Hollywood pilots, plus a few good books on individual personalities. But as far as I know, no one has yet tried to put it all together between two covers—the dramatic history of flying for the movies, how it began, where the planes and pilots come from, and what the opportunities are today for young starry-eyed fliers just now testing their wings.

I should hasten to add that the Hollywood pilot is not a vanishing breed, nor has he or she been totally relegated to the legion of forgotten. No indeed. Movieland of the Air, an impressive, colorful collection of historical aircraft and aviation artifacts used in motion pictures, plus a showcase of related memorabilia, serves as a living memorial to anyone who ever climbed into a cockpit for a flying "gag" —the Hollywood vernacular for stunt. Located at John Wayne Airport in Orange County, California, it is a special tribute to its founders, Paul Mantz and Frank Tallman, two legendary movie pilots who were killed in separate crashes.

In due course Movieland of the Air may become an even greater monument to their memory, as well as to the memory of all who flew for the films. The management of Tallmantz Aviation, which operates the museum, has high hopes of its becoming a major attraction at the proposed Aero World, a $75 million, 342-acre aviation-theme park in California, near Miramar Mesa, or "Miramesa" for short.

Other aviation museums also feature a particular airplane or two that appeared in some well-known motion picture or television production. The most notable, perhaps, include the 1917 Curtiss-JN-4D "Jenny" (N5391) and a 1918 Standard J-1 (2826D) on display at the San Diego Aero-Space Museum in Balboa Park, which, like the legendary phoenix of ancient Egyptian mythology, literally rose from its own ashes following a tragic and costly fire. Both the Jenny and Standard were flown in *It's a Mad, Mad, Mad, Mad World* and *The Spirit of St. Louis*.

The Experimental Aircraft Association's outstanding museum at Hales Corner, Wisconsin, exhibits 180 airplanes, 75 percent of which are operational, including three that "played" in pictures—a Grumman J2F "Duck" of *Murphy's War*; a German Messerschmitt Bf-109 from *Battle of Britain*, and a North American T-6 trainer modified to look like a Japanese Zero for *Tora! Tora! Tora!*

Three replicas of the famous Ryan-built monoplane NX-211 that Charles Lindbergh flew nonstop from New York to Paris in 1927 were constructed for the movie *The Spirit of St. Louis*, starring James Stewart in the title role. One is suspended inside a main terminal building at Lambert-St. Louis International Airport. Another is displayed at the Greenfield Village and Henry Ford Museum in Dearborn, Michigan. The third is housed at Nassau County's Cradle of Aviation Museum at Hempstead, Long Island, New York. And there are several other reproductions on show around the country. The original NX-211, of course, hangs proudly in the Smithsonian Institution's National Air and Space Museum, Washington, D.C.

But the story on the following pages is primarily a story of people—of the aviators and the aerobats who have been risking their necks (and indeed their butts) for filmmakers ever since the movies' earliest days. For when it comes to cinematic thrills and chills, the heart-stopping excitement generated by gyrating, flip-flopping airplanes is mighty hard to beat. In fact, it's the most dangerous flying of all.

Shooting aviation movies is also a hair-raising—and complex—business; therefore, considerable attention has been given the adventurous aerial cameramen. Few take up this hazardous type of cinematography, and those who do enjoy a virtual monopoly on the craft because of the technical skill, cool nerve, and extensive training necessary. They, too, deserve a heaping share of recognition.

Without the generous help of many noble friends, associates, and organizations, this book would have been impossible. They know who they are, and they know they have our never-ending gratitude. But we do want to extend our very special thanks to several very special people who were particularly helpful:

Don Dwiggins, author of hundreds of magazine articles and many books on aviation, biographer of Paul Mantz, a former newspaperman and an active pilot, including some movie stunt flying of his own . . . .

Art Ronnie, also a veteran newspaperman, columnist and studio publicist, now with Columbia Pictures Television; a published writer who is, without question, the foremost authority on Ormer Locklear . . . .

Martin Caidin, prolific author of more than 120 books on aviation and space, a treasure chest of source material, and a fellow airman whose love of the sky is matched only by the exciting way he tells it . . . .

Joe Christy, award-winning author and longtime editor of TAB's Modern Aviation Series, who led us through our first book and talked us into doing this one; a good friend whose advice and counsel we value highly . . . .

Frank Pine, president of Tallmantz Aviation, ex-Navy patrol plane commander, an experienced test pilot, skilled in motion picture and aerial camera flying; a tall, grizzled veteran who knows his business well . . . .

Editor Steve Mesner of TAB, a punctilious stylist and meticulous researcher; his keen personal interest in this work and strict attention to detail contributed much to shaping the finished product . . . .

And my coauthor Maxine, a devoted wife, my chief critic and forever companion in this adventurous world; without her constant inspiration and enthusiastic support I doubt if I could have undertaken a project of this magnitude.

This modest effort, then, is our salute to the Hollywood pilots wherever they are, living or dead. Theirs is truly an honorable, highly specialized profession. In fact, it might be best described as an original American art form— one which millions of screen fans around the world hope and pray will long endure.

Jim Greenwood

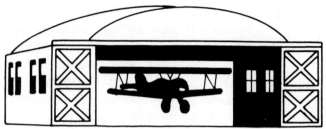

Chapter 1

Birth of the Air Epic

Toward the close of the 19th century, scientists and experimenters on both sides of the Atlantic were in hot pursuit of two new technologies—one involving human flight, the other "moving" pictures. Curiously, in a diversely industrialized world the two objectives had much in common; ultimately their interrelationship would prove key to the success and perfection of each.

Long before that, however, the gifted 15th century Italian genius Leonardo da Vinci had investigated virtually every field of science, including aeronautics and photography. He actually designed a man-powered flying machine based on bird flight; a parachute; and a *camera obscura*, a little box having a lens or small hole through which light from an external object enters to form an image on the opposite wall. But his concept that man could flap the wings of an ornithopter and fly would prove impractical. (Today a man can briefly propel himself in the air only because of ultralight materials available.)

Yet it is no mere coincidence that birds would play a major role in the development of both the airplane and the motion picture. Man had dreamed of emulating the birds for centuries, but until the gliding experiments of Mouillard, Hargrave, Lilienthal, and Pilcher abroad and Chanute, Montgomery, and the Wright brothers in America, he hadn't come close. While all the experimenters had watched birds fly, only Wilbur and Orville Wright had *perceived* that there were two distinct forms of bird flight—the flapping wing variety and soaring. They saw promise in the latter.

Indeed, the evolutionary parallels leading to the invention of the airplane and the discovery of cinematography are not only extraordinary, they are positively uncanny. Birds, toys, and unbridled curiosity were threads in the fabric of both. It is likely that either one would have succeeded on its own, but there is no doubt that one's progress complemented and supplemented the other's, not only in the early formative years, but in more modern times as well. Each is a unique form of *communication*, functioning independently or in combination (the airplane for a camera platform or movies for flight research, as examples).

Actually, the motion picture evolved from the fusion of three separate mechanical interests: the so-called persistence-of-vision toys, still photography, and mechanized audience entertainment devices. The persistence of vision toy capitalized on the physiological fact that the brain retains the images of the eye for an instant longer than the eye actually records them. Such retention allows a series of separate pictures to blend into one another and appear as a fluid and continuous action. It is an optical illusion essential to motion pictures, which are simply a synthesis of individual still photographs or frames.

This formed the basis of many 19th century toys, most of them some kind of circular revolving drum or disc on which were mounted individually drawn figures, each in a slightly different phase of movement. By spinning the disc or drum, the inanimate still pictures came to moving life.

Toys, including model planes, also served as patterns for the early designs of man-carrying flying machines. Toy helicopters, in fact, can be traced back to the Middle Ages. But it was the French experimenter Alphonse Pénaud who, in 1870, introduced twisted rubber bands to power model aircraft, his first configured as a helicopter. Then in 1871 he brought out his elastic-powered "Planophore" monoplane, the world's first inherently stable aircraft model. Interestingly, the Pénaud model is not unlike the rubber band designs of today.

It was a Pénaud toy that fascinated the Wright brothers as small boys, but the Wrights' interests were wide-ranging. As they grew older, they (Orville in particular), became enamored with photography, a hobby that would serve them well during their flying experiments. The brothers recorded on film just about every major milestone in their efforts to conquer the sky, including the immortal shot of Orville leaving the ground for the first time at Kill Devil Hill, North Carolina.

Orville and Wilbur were also fond of serious reading, including such heavy fare as Plutarch's *Lives*, Boswell's *Life of Johnson*, and Green's *History of England*. They also perused

Orville Wright set up the camera, but John T. Daniels of the Kill Devil Life Saving Station actually snapped this historic photograph of the world's first flight. (Library of Congress)

Eadweard Muybridge's still photos of figures in motion were the precursors of motion pictures. His work led to breakthroughs by another pioneer, Etienne-Jules Marey. (George Eastman House)

two encyclopedias, the *Britannica* and *Chambers*, but one of the most important volumes to their later work was a book about birds titled *Animal Mechanism* by Etienne-Jules Marey, a professor at the College of France and member of the French Academy of Medicine. First published in Paris, its English translation appeared in London in 1874 and in the United States in 1887.

Marey based his book on his personal observations of real birds, but he also simulated the feathered creatures in his laboratory. He developed various shaped, birdlike bodies and suspended them within a large enclosed chamber or wind tunnel. Then he photographed the flow of air over the different surfaces by blowing smoke (to make the air currents visible) against the objects in the chamber. As a result, Marey created a new method of aerodynamic research which would prove of great value to later experimenters.

Inspired by the innovative work of Eadweard Muybridge, who in the late 1800s photographed animal movements in a series of still pictures, Marey also made rapid-sequence photos of birds in actual flight. These efforts, coupled with his studies in aerodynamics, would lay the foundation for cinematography. Marey's experiments were a factor in Wilbur and Orville Wright's decision to build a wind tunnel in 1901, which helped them solve the secret of powered flight.

Incredibly, by the time the brothers finally flew in 1903, one of America's most distinguished scientists and inventors, Thomas Alva Edison, had already publicly stated that flight was impossible. Edison, whose forays into many fields were continuing evidence of a da Vinci-like breadth of mind, had stopped his own work on a flying machine after concluding that successful flight would require an engine capable of producing at least 50 horsepower and weighing less than 40 pounds. At that stage of engine development (1880s), such technology was still years in the future.

But along with many other splendid inventions, such as the incandescent lamp and the phonograph, Edison is credited with developing the first workable motion picture camera in America to use strip film. Called Edison's Strip Kinetograph, the new machine came out in 1889. The film it used ran through the camera horizontally.

The introduction of theatrical projection for shared audiences at the turn of the century was the final element necessary for the advent of the "movies," as distinct from peep shows and parlor toys that had come before. Although the novelty of the one-reeler at local nickelodeons was already beginning to wear off, Edwin S. Porter, Edison's director of production, conceived the first feature length film that told a story—*The Great Train Robbery*. It was an instant sensation and remained for years a staple of the burgeoning storefront nickelodeon trade. Thus the motion picture as a medium of entertainment was assured.

It should be noted that *The Great Train Robbery*, which epitomized a new wave of filmmaking, was completed in 1903 and copyrighted December 1 of that year. Less than three weeks later—on December 17, near Kitty Hawk—the Wright brothers were to make history's first powered, controlled, sustained flight in a heavier-than-air machine. (In fact, they made four flights that day: the first, with Orville up, covered 120 feet in 12 seconds; Wilbur flew the fourth a distance of 852

Orville and Wilbur Wright with their second powered machine at Huffman Prairie, Simms Station, near Dayton. They did most of their testing there after Kitty Hawk. (Library of Congress)

Spain's King Alphonso XIII, with Wilbur Wright, did not go up, but in 1909 a Universal News cameraman accompanied Wilbur and took the first movies from a plane in flight. (Library of Congress)

feet in 59 seconds.) Edison's first adventure motion picture and the Wrights' first adventure aloft in a powered machine would each have a profound effect on our way of life.

On April 24, 1909, near the end of a highly successful tour of Europe, the Wrights demonstrated their plane to King Victor Emmanuel III of Italy at a small field on the outskirts of Rome. A highlight of the afternoon's activities came when Wilbur took a Universal News cameraman along on one of his flights. It marked the first time in history that motion pictures had ever been taken from an airplane in flight.

Because the quality of the cinematography was so good and the aerial scenes of the countryside so spectacular prints of the film were widely distributed. From that point on, the flying machine and the motion picture were forever wedded.

The Wrights had achieved in four and a half short years what the greatest minds of the world had failed to accomplish in all history. The story of their remarkable achievement was the subject of a two-hour television special aired over the NBC network on December 17, 1978—the 75th anniversary of powered flight. A dramatization titled *The Winds of Kitty*

A full-scale Wright replica built by Tom and Bob Valentine helped recreate history's first flight for NBC-TV's *The Winds of Kitty Hawk*, a two-hour ITT special. (Frank Goodman Associates)

Michael Moriarity, left, played Wilbur Wright, and David Huffman, Orville. But producers of the NBC special took liberties with history in an attempt to make a better drama. (Frank Goodman Associates)

Hawk, the show received mixed reviews and evoked considerable controversy. Critics acclaimed the cinematography but condemned the story line for "grossly distorting" the facts. It was another case of rewriting history in the name of entertainment.

The flights in 1903 (and in the next two years) were reported with little fanfare; the world did not know of the Wrights' triumph until 1906. Had their earlier flights been widely publicized, the evolution of the airplane might have been accelerated. As it happened, the pooling of basic ideas, American and European, did not become general until 1909.

Meanwhile, as word of flying spread over both continents, men and women of all backgrounds—sportsmen and sculptors, lawyers and businessmen—were drawn to the new "sport" and adventure in the sky. Individually, these pioneers were as diverse in temperament as in background. Collectively they were like a fraternal order, a band of brothers bound together by the exhilarating challenge of flight. Again and again they risked their necks to win the plaudits of the earth-bound admirers. In rapid succession they set new marks for speed, distance, altitude and duration, smashing bones as often as records.

Pioneers in a dozen countries or more fashioned and flew (or attempted to fly), all manner of peculiar-looking contraptions. And while there was by now no question that the Wright brothers had led the pack, other serious contenders were fast emerging, spurred

Michael Moriarity, unfortunately, was not a very believable Wilbur Wright in *The Winds of Kitty Hawk*. Location filming was done at San Luis Obispo, California. (Frank Goodman Associates)

This 1909 Wright Military Flyer marked the beginning of the present-day U.S. Air Force. The Army used early aircraft for camera platforms as well as weapons. (Smithsonian NASM)

on by wealthy and influential sponsors who posted attractive cash prizes and other awards for pacemaking and record-breaking feats.

On July 25, 1909, Louis Blériot, one of the few persons to witness Wilbur Wright's first flight in Europe (at Le Mans, France, August 8, 1908), became the first pilot in history to cross the English Channel in an airplane, signaling that the world's geographical features would no longer be boundaries to men. Flying his Blériot XI he spanned the 25 miles from Calais to Dover in 37 minutes, winning the *London Daily Mail* prize of $5,000. But this was only the beginning.

The public had read about those magnificent men in their flying machines; now suddenly they could watch them in a whole series of races and competitions, fairs, and exhibitions which blossomed in the carefree years before World War I. The international aviation meet at Rheims, France, was the first of the great exhibitions, drawing an estimated crowd of 250,00 people to see such "early birds" as Glenn Curtiss, Léon Delagrange, Henri Farman and the already famous Blériot put their frail machines through their paces. Curtiss, shunning the altitude and distance contests to concentrate on the speed events, won the grand prize—the Gordon Bennett Cup—by flying his souped-up Golden Flyer an average speed of 47 miles an hour over a 20-kilometer course.

Rheims was the lone notable aviation competition in 1909, but the following year numerous air meets burst forth in America and Europe. The competitions at Los Angeles, Boston, and Belmont Park in Long Island, for example, again drew international rosters of aviators, large and celebrity-studded audiences, and the usual number of thrills and spills.

It was truly an adventurous, exciting period of aviation history and undoubtedly inspired the 20th Century-Fox movie entitled *Those Magnificent Men in Their Flying Machines, or: How I Flew from London to Paris in 25 Hours and 11 Minutes.* Released in 1965, the colorful, technically innovative production is a film tribute (though in the form of a comic valentine) to all the daring young men who, at the beginning of the century, bravely took to the air in flying machines of every size, shape, and description. Set in England in 1910, it's a good-natured spoof on the one hand and on the other, a fairly accurate portrayal of pioneer airmen and their primitive aircraft struggling to get and stay airborne.

Those Magnificent Men in Their Flying Machines is the story of the "first international air race across the English Channel." Although it is a work of pure fiction, director Ken Annakin, who collaborated on the screenplay with associate producer Jack Davies, leaned heavily on factual events in recreating the most significant elements and conditions found at the early aviation contests of the time.

As a matter of fact, Annakin had long been considering a serious film on the embryonic days of flying when he discovered Davies was developing an original screenplay treating the comic aspects inherent in the exploits of visionary aviators and their outlandish products. The two joined forces, agreeing on the comic viewpoint, but in an otherwise very lively, hilariously funny script, there's one reflectively profound, thought-provoking bit of dialogue worth noting. Proposing the international air race to British newspaper peer Lord Rawnsley (played by Robert Morley), the dashing English aviator Richard Mays (James Fox) states, "The trouble with aviation today is that too many good ideas are being dissipated in too many aeroplanes. If we could bring together all the different types from all over the world, then everyone could learn from each other."

A balloon duel with blunderbusses was one of the funnier episodes in *Those Magnificent Men in Their Flying Machines*, a humorous movie about an international air race. (20th Century-Fox)

Those Magnificent Men patterned many scenes after actual events in aviation's early years. The world's racetracks often served as stages for the first flying exhibitions. (20th Century-Fox)

Reproductions of the vintage Bristol Boxkite, Bleriot, Demoiselle, Antoinette, Avro Triplane, and the Eardley-Billings biplane shared top billing in *Those Magnificent Men*. (20th Century-Fox)

The picture merits a brief mention at this juncture simply because it depicts, even if humorously, that romantic point in time when flying and films were both in their infancy, and it represents the type of aviation movie that always faces staggering technical problems in achieving realism. Bringing back the beauty and excitement of the Edwardian era alone proved both a challenge and an inspiration to producer Stan Margulies and his associates.

There were more than the usual number of difficulties. For the British "aerodrome" setting, for instance, a site had to be found at which scenes could be photographed from the air in almost any direction without exposing TV aerials, electric wires, paved roads, or other details inconsistent with 1910.

Sharing top billing with the stars (Stuart Whitman, Sarah Miles, Morley and Fox), of course, were the planes themselves. The aircraft recreated for the film were authentic reproductions of 1910 originals. Even the more whimsically designed types, which were shown for the first time on the screen in *Those Magnificent Men in Their Flying Machines*, were constructed from original drawings dug out of air archives in London and Paris. To insure their authenticity, Elmo Williams (then chief of European production for Twentieth Century-Fox), engaged a trustee of the Shuttleworth Collection at Biggleswade to act as aeronautical advisor, Commodore Allen Wheeler.

In one detail the reproduction did vary from the originals. Instead of assuming the added expense of having a machine shop build

General configuration of the Phoenix Flyer in the movie *Those Magnificent Men* resembled in some detail Henry Farman's successful machines of the 1910 period. (20th Century-Fox)

Sir Percy Ware-Armitage (Terry-Thomas) hauls his wrecked Avro home by horse and wagon, recalling similar real-life scenes in man's long struggle to conquer the skies. (20th Century-Fox)

the tooling necessary to turn out exact duplicates of the old engines, the small planes mounted geared Volkswagen motors; the larger used Rolls-Royce powerplants. They were actually no more powerful than the handmade engines of 1910, but they were more dependable.

Even so, the reproductions could not get off the ground with any degree of safety in winds stronger than 10 to 15 miles per hour. This situation gave rise to a new cry from assistant director Clive Reed who kidded the film crews and players by shouting, "Ready! Quiet! Roll 'em! *Hold your breath!* Action!"

Although the producers took numerous precautions in the interest of safety, there was still considerable danger in flying the planes used for the movie. Interestingly, each of the six aircraft that did most of the flying had more stand-ins than the stars. Stand-in number one remained in readiness to avoid delaying production in the event of any mishap involving its "star" counterpart. Stand-in number two was especially built so that it could be taken apart in sections for close-up filming. None of the pilots who flew the planes had stand-ins, however. (Luckily, none were needed.)

Not generally known is the fact that the pilot who tested the smaller machines and flew most of the aerobatics required of them in the film was a woman—Joan Hughes, one of England's leading test pilots. Miss Hughes was called in after the studio's Demoiselle mono-plane failed to rise more than a few feet off the ground when flown by its builder, Douglas Bianchi.

It was a knotty problem. Bianchi had constructed the plane, a replica of a model designed and flown by Alberto Santos-Dumont in 1909, in minute detail from drawings and photographs stored at the *Musée de l'Air* in Paris. Finally, the mystery of the balky plane was solved after further research uncovered the fact that Santos-Dumont himself weighed only 110 pounds, whereas aircraftsman Bianchi tipped the scales at 182. With Miss Hughes at the controls, the little Demoiselle performed beautifully. Like Santos-Dumont, she also weighed only 110 pounds.

There were many sets for the film, but the one used most was "Brookley Aerodrome," a field of approximately 80 acres. It was actually Booker Air Field in England's lush Buckingham countryside, which served as a Royal Air Force base in World War II. The fictional "Brookley," however, was patterned after Brooklands, hub of British aviation activity in pre-World War I days, a time when several European nations, most nobably France, were beginning to develop airplanes for military use.

With the outbreak of hostilities in 1914, America hastened to proclaim its neutrality. Yet because of its melting pot population with strong ties to Europe, the United States could not very well stay indifferent to the struggle overseas. Although sentiment in some areas favored the Central or Axis Powers, the great majority of the American people supported the cause of the Allies.

Meanwhile, few inventions appearing at the beginning of this century had captured the American public so completely as the "moving picture show"—it seemed to embrace and exude even more magic than the airplane. (There's still a hint of magic in the word "movies" even today.) But the war in Europe

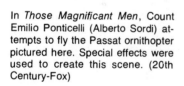

In *Those Magnificent Men*, Count Emilio Ponticelli (Alberto Sordi) attempts to fly the Passat ornithopter pictured here. Special effects were used to create this scene. (20th Century-Fox)

probably gave more impetus to advancing the state of the art in aeronautics—and to a certain extent, cinematography as well—than any other single factor. By the time America joined the Allies in 1917, airplanes had semi-enclosed cockpits and cowlings, bristled with armament, and in some configurations could fly at speeds approaching 200 miles an hour.

The newsreels had already arrived; in fact, Albert E. Smith and J. Stuart Blackton of the Vitagraph Company filmed the charge up San Juan Hill, during the Spanish-American War of 1898, while actually on location in Cuba. But they also had no compunctions about staging the battle of Santiago Bay in a New York bathtub; Smith turned the crank as Mrs. Blackton puffed smoke into the lens and her husband manipulated the bobbing paper cut-

outs of the battle fleet. The public accepted the phony footage in all innocence and American producers soon offered the Boer War as shot in New Jersey and the Russo-Japanese War restaged at Verbeck's Japanese Gardens in Manlius, New York.

Film crews frequently risked their lives photographing World War I, although some of their battle scenes, too, were staged and then presented as reality. Movies of aerial combat were difficult to fake, however, at least until years later when the science of optics and special effects had become more sophisticated in the land of make-believe. But to the practiced eye even today, as then, Hollywood hokum in aviation film is quickly and easily discernible.

When war first erupted in Europe, a

People everywhere cheered those bold adventurers who, at the beginning of the century, risked life and limb taking to the air in machines of outlandish design. (20th Century-Fox)

William F. "Buffalo Bill" Cody's Wild West Show was first captured on movie film in the late 1890s. Cody is pictured in 1915 with another showman, pilot Art Smith.

number of American volunteers rushed to enlist in Allied units such as the Foreign Legion, which did not require them to give up U.S. citizenship. A few young men, enthralled by stories they had heard about flying, signed up with Britain's Royal Flying Corps (now the RAF) or the French Army's air service. Out of the French air squadrons would come the first all-American fighting unit in the war—the *Lafayette Escadrille*.

There were seven pilots in the charter group: Norman Prince, Elliott Cowdin, Victor Chapman, William Thaw, Kiffin Rockwell, Bert Hall and James McConnell. They were soon joined by others whose names are prominent in Lafayette history, including Raoul Lufbery, Clyde Balsley, Dudley Hill, Harold Willis, James Norman Hall (no relation to Bert Hall) and Didier Masson. All told there were 43 American fliers in the squadron. Two of

them would go on to make their mark in motion pictures—director William Wellman and writer John Monk Saunders.

From the moment the Lafayette Escadrille went into action it was a living legend. While the lives of the airmen weren't always as glamorous as they seemed, American reporters, eager to infuse their dispatches home with excitement and adventure, often exaggerated the squadron's exploits. The newsreel coverage also perpetuated the myth that combat flying was filled with romance and glory. Yet clearly the encounters of Lafayette pilots with the enemy provided some of the best air stories to come out of World War I.

Scenes of high and low flying airplanes arcing through all kinds of crazy maneuvers were not exactly new to American theatergoers. Months before U.S. pilots fought in French battle skies, enterprising promoters like William H. Pickens gained broad public exposure for their aviator clients on the prewar fair and carnival circuit. Pickens fancied himself as the world's greatest press agent in those halcyon days, possibly with some justification. Coincidentally, Pickens began his publicity career by selling cylinder phonographs for Thomas Edison, whose pioneering in motion pictures was already widely known.

Bill Pickens managed Lincoln Beachey, at one time the brightest star in the Curtiss Exhibition Company's galaxy of professional pilots. Between Pickens' talent for ballyhoo and Lincoln's flying skill, Beachey soon became America's first barnstorming hero. It was Pickens who devised the early automobile-versus-airplane race, pitting cigar-chomping racing driver Barney Oldfield against the nattily attired flier. With the willing help of newsreel cameramen, Pickens made the Oldfield-Beachey contests into county fair classics.

As far as is known, Pickens had nothing to do with the one daring "flying" stunt that, according to Lowell Thomas, long the pillar of Fox Movietone News and perhaps the best-known newscaster who ever lived, "launched the newsreel industry in the United States." Contriving the stunt strictly for publicity, a parachutist named Rodman Law took a swan dive off the Statue of Liberty. The jump was an artistic failure, said Thomas, because Law's chute opened late and he barely escaped with his life. But four cameramen were on hand to film the event. Thus the newsreel was on its way to becoming an American institution—and as much a part of the movies as buttered popcorn.

For the movie storyteller as well as the photojournalist, aviation has provided an abundance of source material ever since the first public demonstrations of the Wright brothers were recorded on film over 70 years ago. (Their flights in 1909 at Fort Myer, Virginia, and in France and Italy the same year received extensive newsreel coverage.) Moreover, the impact of aeronautics on western society had been felt almost immediately by the movie industry, likewise young and growing.

Early story film found war backgrounds effective (though expensive) variations on standard plots, such as the "good guys/bad guys" theme. The one-reelers of pioneer movie-maker D. W. Griffith contained a number of Civil War titles (*The Battle* in 1911, for example) that served as sketches for more important work later. But it was Griffith's *Birth of a Nation* in 1915 that first startled audiences with the spectacle of massed columns and the panoramic sweep of smoke-filled battlescapes. The motion picture had abruptly come of age.

The next year the real war became a topic of more immediate importance. Yet fighting on

Lincoln Beachey, flying a Curtiss Pusher, and Barney Oldfield, lower right, thrilled fair crowds coast to coast with their famous automobile versus airplane races and stunts.

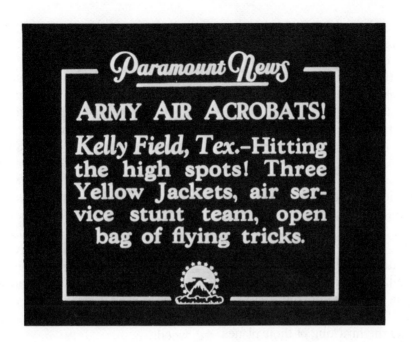

Paramount News

ARMY AIR ACROBATS!

Kelly Field, Tex.-Hitting the high spots! Three Yellow Jackets, air service stunt team, open bag of flying tricks.

First movies of airplanes flying successfully were made in 1908. For the next 50 years, aviation events and machines were newsreel topics in the nation's movie houses. Army "Yellow Jackets" in Boeing P-12s comprised one of the early military flight demonstration teams preceding today's USAF Thunderbirds and Navy Blue Angels.

land, which could only be described as horrific, lacked the glamour sought by studio moguls. Consequently, the image of airmen as chivalrous "knights of the air," duelling individually and cleanly far above the dreadful trenches, gave filmmakers the grist of their screenwriting mill. By 1918 the real career of the Lafayette Escadrille had ceased, its identity and personnel now merged with the other American squadrons then in France. Soon the likes of Eddie Rickenbacker and Frank Luke were also being lionized as gallant heroes of modern warfare.

Oddly, one of the first feature-length movie stories with an aviation theme wasn't a war picture at all. Produced by the Universal Film Company in 1919, its slim plot revolved around the adventures of pilots in the U.S. Air Mail Service and the hijacking of their planes by a mysterious band of criminals. It was a thriller set in the future—1930. And though it may not rank as one of the great air epics of all time, the film did forecast a day when aviation would become an essential mode of transportation.

The picture also anticipated a day of air piracy, proclaiming "we shall have highwaymen of the clouds and society bandits plying their trade in the air."

Universal president Carl Laemmle chucked the title originally proposed for the picture, *Cassidy of the Air Lanes.* Instead he decided to call it *The Great Air Robbery*, perhaps because the title of the industry's first financially successful story film—*The Great Train Robbery*—was still relatively fresh in the public mind. And for the leading role studio chief Laemmle chose a flamboyant ex-Army aviator turned barnstormer whose feats of derring-do had not gone unnoticed by Hollywood.

His name: Ormer Leslie Locklear, a daredevil's daredevil whose time was running out.

Chapter 2

"But the Name Is Ormer"

They were indeed a breed apart, the barnstorming fliers of yesteryear. They walked wings, jumped parachutes and stunted airplanes in a hell-for-leather fashion that fractured just about every law of physics known to science. Daring beyond belief, these intrepid members of the helmet, goggles and scarf set are best described as boldly rugged individualists. Except for one important fact: All shared an engaging quality vital to their trade—*showmanship*.

During aviation's formative years, an incredulous, awestruck public identified death-defying aeronauts by a variety of colloquialisms, such as "flying vagabonds," "winged gypsies," "aerial nomads," "stunt merchants," "the incorrigibles" or just plain "mavericks." But in modern aeronautical lexicon, one nickname has endured almost since the day man first flew. It was borrowed from the touring theater, which prevailed during that period of American history . . . .

Barnstormer.

No other word better fits the exclusive coterie of pioneer aviators who literally placed flying on the public doorstep. Alone or in groups (the flying circus), barnstormers chased a dream coast to coast, border to bor-

der. They crisscrossed the country in ungainly craft made of wood, wire and linen, their box-like machines often held together by little more than a lick, promise and prayer.

Back in those days whenever and wherever a barnstormer descended, crowds of curious townspeople would race to the landing site, usually some local farmer's pasture. In this way the miracle of flight was exposed to the grass roots of America. All this occurred at a time when, because of doubting skepticism, fear or ignorance, the general public saw the airplane as having little practical value. Further, the lure of the early aerial sideshows was all too often the possibility of an accident—the chance that blood would be spilled in some new and bizarre way—and sometimes the spectators staring into the sky got what they came for.

In the pre-World War I era, the biggest names in exhibition aviation belonged to the traveling teams organized by Glenn Curtiss, the Wrights, and John Moisant. Curtiss' team boasted the great Lincoln Beachey, Eugene Ely, J. C. "Bud" Mars, and Charles Willard. The Wrights' company starred Walter Brookins, Arch Hoxsey, Frank Coffyn, and Ralph Johnstone. Moisant had an international

America's top stunt pilot during flying's infancy was Lincoln Beachey, whose performances nationwide were frequent newsreel subjects. He crashed to his death in 1915. (Hillary Beachey collection)

Ormer Locklear was born October 28, 1891, in the small Texas town of Como, Hopkins County, near Fort Worth. His penchant for stunting began with motorcycles and continued with airplanes after he joined the U.S. Army Air Service at the age of 26. A lean, hard-muscled bundle of energy, Locklear was destined to become the undisputed king of the daredevils and the darling of the movie world.

"To Locklear, more than anyone else, can be credited the tremendous boom in barnstorming that captured America in the twenties," states Art Ronnie, Ormer's authoritative biographer. "He made wing-walking an art. When he was the first man to change from one plane to another in midair, he amazed the world, even though most credited him with more guts than brains. It was his

Promoter William H. "Bill" Pickens, left with Ormer Locklear. Pickens also represented Lincoln Beachey, Barney Oldfield and football great Harold "Red" Grange. (Art Ronnie collection)

team that included the Frenchman Roland Garros, first man to fly across the Mediterranean (1913) and later the first flier to score an aerial combat victory by firing through his plane's propeller.

Following the war many former service pilots and civilians, some of whom had taught military flying, bought surplus planes (such as the Curtiss JN-4D Jenny, a Canadian version called the Canuck, and the Standard J-1 trainer) for a fraction of their original cost. Filled with exuberance and unbridled optimism for the future of flying, they struck out to "sell" aviation in every corner of the land. But the expected resurgence of barnstorming got off to a wobbly start.

That is, until Ormer Locklear roared into view.

Known as the "man who walked on wings," Ormer Locklear was fearless in the air. Here he stands on top of a Curtiss JN-4D in flight. (Peter M. Bowers collection)

startling stunt work in the air, copied by many others, that gave that extra dash and thrill to movie serials just beginning their greatest era."

Locklear scrambled all over an airplane in flight like a human squirrel. He developed his ability to wing-walk and change planes while flying Curtiss Jennies in the service in Texas. In fact, in 1918 he and two close flying buddies, Milton "Skeets" Elliott and James Frew, actually performed such razzle-dazzle demonstrations under Army auspices. Because there had been so many fatal crashes at Texas flying fields, the Army saw Locklear's stunts as a morale booster. It hoped "Lock's" lack of fear and obvious faith in the Jenny's flying qualities would instill the same in other pilots.

Ormer's desire for thrills quickly led to more daring antics. He found them in changing from one plane to another in full flight, a risky stunt which he first executed on November 8,

1918. Shortly after the signing of the Armistice three days later, Frew returned to civilian life. With the war over, Locklear and Elliott, who had become squadron commanders, were now stunt fliers first and militarists second. They promptly looked for someone to replace Frew and finally selected Lt. Shirley J. Short, one of the most able flight instructors in Texas.

During the next year, Lock refined his midair transfer by stepping from the wing of one Jenny to another as the planes flew parallel with each other. He was also first to use the rope ladder, which would become standard equipment among barnstormers.

William H. "Bill" Pickens, who had managed Lincoln Beachey and Barney Oldfield among other aviation and auto racing celebrities, latched onto Locklear, Elliott, and Short when the trio left the Army in May 1919. In Locklear, particularly, the promoter's instincts told him he had the hottest property in show business. Pickens purchased three new Canucks from the Curtiss factory in Canada and sent the three airmen on a national barnstorming tour. He called the new show the Locklear Flying Circus.

They opened May 16, 1919, at the Uniontown Speedway in Pennsylvania. It marked the first public exhibition of Locklear's thrilling plane-changing act, but there was more, much more. First, Lock would hang by his legs from the landing gear, then dangle by one arm from the skid bar at the tip of the bottom wing. Next he would inch his way along the fuselage to the tail where he would sit waving to the crowd as pilot Short flew the plane past the grandstand. After an agonizing crawl back to the front end,

he would flirt with death by doing a headstand directly behind the whirling propeller.

But before the excited spectators had a chance to regain their composure, Skeets Elliott would bring his plane up perilously close to Short's, a six-foot rope ladder dangling beneath. Everywhere the fliers appeared the reaction to what happened next was the same. Typical is the *Illinois State Journal's* description of Ormer's performance in Springfield:

"Locklear's plane-changing feat requires about 10 minutes from the moment the machines begin to jockey for position until he is safe in the seat of the other airplane. During that time, silence prevails among the crowd, no matter how huge. It seems as though

Billed as the Locklear Flying Circus, left to right: Milton Elliot, Ormer Locklear, and Shirley Short. Note Locklear's resemblance to Clark Gable. (Locklear family collection)

Rope ladder, a standard piece of barnstorming equipment right up to the present day, was first used by Ormer Locklear. Here Eddie Green grabs Piper Cub's ladder.

everyone holds his breath. As he makes the change, the crowd bursts into a spontaneous cheer that does not die until the intrepid fellow is landed in front of the grandstand."

Thousands witnessed these acts of aerial wizardry at fairgrounds and expositions all over America. Some fairs paid Locklear a fee of $3,000 a *day* (as personal services agent, Pickens pocketed a neat 50 percent) and considerably higher sums were paid for a week of exhibitions. It was a lot of money for a flier at a time when most pilots just out of the war were lucky to attract a crowd of farmers in some lonely meadow. Bill Pickens summed up his philosophy of values in an interview published

June 15, 1919 in the *Erie Daily Times*, Erie, Pennsylvania:

"We can't be bothered with flying sodbusters at five bucks a hop; Locklear is giving them something that no one else can. And until someone can do what he's doing, I'm taking them for everything I can."

Just the day before, Ormer had attempted his first car-to-plane change on the Erie fairgrounds track. The heat was oppressive—and Lock's underestimating of a basic aerodynamic principle almost cost him his life. As car and plane raced around the oval track, he stood up and grabbed the last rung of the ladder dangling from the Jenny flying above. But his weight

23

On the studio set of *The Skywayman*: William H. Pickens, left, Ormer Locklear's press agent; Locklear, and H. K. Shellaby, Ormer's business manager. (Locklear family collection)

pulled the plane down and in the scorchingly hot summer air the plane lost much of its lifting power. Lock was suddenly in danger of being dragged along the ground directly in the path of the speeding auto.

Ormer made a split-second decision and let go. The Jenny shot into the air and Locklear rolled out of the way, just as the car turned sharply to avoid his tumbling body, crashing through a guard rail. Lock's instant reflex averted a possible tragedy that could have killed all three men. Interestingly, Ormer didn't try the car-to-plane transfer again until he hit Hollywood.

As a devil-may-care barnstormer mock-ing death at every performance, along with the increasing popularity of aviation, it was inevitable that Ormer Leslie Locklear would soon find his way into motion pictures. Pioneer producer Carl Laemmle of Universal, first to sign the flier, said "Locklear's films marked the beginning of a regular and extensive use of airplanes by movie companies."

When Locklear arrived in Los Angeles he was besieged by reporters. Like most of the press around the country, they couldn't spell or pronounce Ormer's name correctly, not being quite sure whether it was Omar or Omer. (Who ever heard of Ormer?) Consequently, Hollywood would know Ormer as *Omar* (which, come to think of it, might have been more appropriate for this new environment). In his excellent work *Locklear: The Man Who Walked on Wings,* published by A. S. Barnes and Company in 1973, author Art Ronnie recounts a delightful exchange recalling the difficulties with Ormer's name:

"Is it a dangerous trick to jump from one plane to another several thousand feet in the air, Omar?" asked one reporter.

"It's no trick and far from dangerous. I wouldn't do the feat if it was dangerous. And the name is Ormer."

"How long will you continue to do it?"

"Until I die of old age."

"Omar, why did you change from dropping from one plane to another for the rope climb?"

"A man is really foolish to risk his life and I didn't believe in taking unnecessary chances. But the name is *Ormer.*"

Contrary to what he told reporters, Locklear's motto was "Safety Second" and he indeed lived up to it. Yet he scoffed at people who called him a fatalist and those who knew him best were quick to confirm that Lock would rarely take an unnecessary chance. But being basically a showman, it's only natural that he would become caught up in the world of make-believe. It is also natural that he would attract people like Mary Pickford's brother Jack, who also had a wild flying streak in him. They met at Cecil B. DeMille's Mercury Avia-

King of the daredevils, Ormer Locklear skyrocketed to unprecedented success. Here he hangs by an arm from a Curtiss Jenny in 1919. (Peter M. Bowers collection)

Tony Lynch, Jeanie Macpherson and Cecil B. DeMille in 1918. Lynch, along with Al Wilson, taught DeMille to fly. Macpherson was DeMille's close associate. (Cecil B. DeMille Trust)

tion Company, where Jack Pickford was learning to fly; soon they were inseparable friends.

DeMille, by the way, operated a couple of airports in the Los Angeles area in the early postwar years. Too old at 36 to enter the Army Air Service as a student pilot, he learned to fly in 1917 anyway, getting his instruction from Al Wilson, another stunter who later flew for motion pictures. He established Mercury Aviation in 1918 and the following year started a local airline.

Apparently, cavorting about the sky in a Curtiss Jenny held more fascination for DeMille than producing and directing motion pic-

tures. At least that was what his film industry associates thought. Mercury Aviation was, therefore, short-lived. But while it flourished, operations (at three DeMille Fields) sold rides, taught flying, ran California's first commercial airline, and provided the planes, pilots and movie locations for a wide array of Hollywood productions.

One competitor, Syd Chaplin (screen comedian Charlie's airminded brother), owned the "Chaplin Aerodrome" directly across the street from DeMille Field Number 2 at the corner of Wilshire Boulevard and Crescent Avenue (now Fairfax). This particular airport was the center of intense aviation activity in the early 1920s.

Having already acquired a number of war surplus airplanes, including several Curtiss Jennies and Canadian Canucks, Mercury added five revolutionary all-metal Junkers-Larsen JL-6 passenger models to its fleet for airline service. Captain Edward V. "Eddie" Ricken-

At Ascot Park Speedway July 20, 1919, Cecil B. DeMille pits his JN-4D against race driver Eddie Hearne's Chevrolet and riding mechanic Harry Hartz. (Cecil B. DeMille Trust)

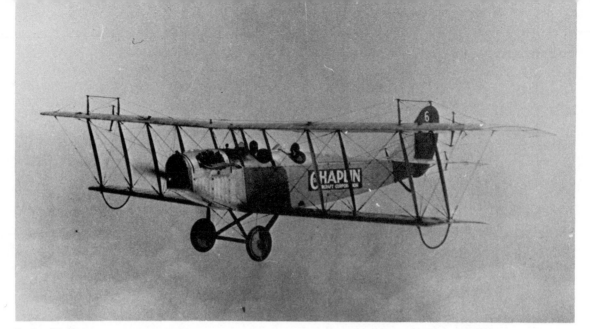

Curtiss JN-4D Jenny operated by Syd Chaplin before Chaplin sold out to Emory Rogers. Chaplin Field, which became Rogers Airport, was scene of many movie stunts. (Francis H. Dean)

Goodyear blimp lands on Mercury Aviation's DeMille Field 2 at Wilshire Boulevard, foreground, and Crescent Avenue, now Fairfax. Hollywood Hills are in background. (Walter Hawkins)

backer delivered one of the new low-wing cabin monoplanes, the first of its type to be operated in the U.S. Although touted as the last word in travel comfort, the JL-6 was a firetrap and would soon be grounded.

In September 1921 Mercury sold out to Emory Rogers, who ran Chaplin's field. The pioneering venture may have been a financial failure, but DeMille, who became one of the greatest studio heads in all history, loved every minute of it. DeMille stopped flying in 1925, at fellow filmmaker Adolph Zukor's insistence, except for a quick turn at the controls of a Lockheed 10 in 1934—under the watchful eye of Paul Mantz. And though he decided he was a better director than a pilot, C. B. De-Mille had definitely made his mark in aviation.

Meanwhile, DeMille Field Number 1 was preparing for location shooting on Ormer Locklear's first picture, *The Great Air Robbery.* A principal source of Mercury's income derived from rival studios renting the DeMille fields and planes for filming movie serials and air epics.

A flying sequence for Harry Houdini's first film, *The Grim Game,* was also shot at DeMille Field Number 2. It very nearly ended in tragedy, and for years the lucky "escape" was credited to the master escape artist himself, who wasn't even there at the time. But the script called for Houdini to drop from one plane into the cockpit of another. According to one report, stuntman Robert Kennedy, a wing-walker doubling for Houdini, got down on his ladder and froze. At that point wind gusts or turbulence shoved the two planes together,

Cecil B. DeMille, center, hand on wing, proudly shows off Mercury Aviation's new all-metal plane in 1920. Note how pilot must hold cabin door open. (Cecil B. DeMille Trust)

This plane rigged for motion picture filming belonged to Emory Rogers, who purchased Syd Chaplin's flying field in 1920. In 1922 Rogers bought out C.B. DeMille. (Art Ronnie collection)

the landing gear of the upper Jenny crunching into the top wing of the lower ship.

Locking wings 2,000 feet in the air, the two Jennies started a double flat spin. They finally broke apart and the pilots managed to land, one with a shattered upper right wing and Kennedy still clinging to his ladder. The other came in with more serious damage and rolled over on its back. Miraculously, all three airmen escaped serious injury.

In the characteristic tradition of filmmaking, director-cameraman Irvin Willat in a third plane kept his head and captured the whole

frightening episode. Without question, his was some of the most remarkable and thrilling action footage ever recorded on film.

The Great Air Robbery would be the first movie made at DeMille Field Number 1, situated at the corner of Melrose and Crescent (now Fairfax) Avenues, Los Angeles. The publicity-minded DeMille took full advantage of it. The planes, field, and hangars were all leased from him. False fronts on the buildings proclaimed they were the property of the "United States Aerial Mail" but DeMille saw that his initials, "CB," appeared not only on the structures, but on the planes used in the picture as well.

Locklear played a pilot in the U.S. Air Mail Service whose antagonists were members of the "Death's Head Squadron," an unscrupulous gang of lawless fliers bent on hijacking shipments of gold sent by air. Several plane changes were slated for the movie, but a plane-to-car transfer easily provided the most exciting and dramatic moment. Recalling his near-disaster with the auto-to-plane change at Erie six weeks earlier, Lock elected to switch the procedure. But this time he practiced the stunt relentlessly on a back lot road before attempting the change in front of the cameras.

Site of the attempt was along Cahuenga Road, a narrow dirt strip running through a pass in the Santa Monica Mountains linking Hollywood with the San Fernando Valley. The first try was so successful that an elated Locklear ordered script changes so he could make a double transfer: plane-to-car; car-to-plane. This he also performed flawlessly. The date: July 26, 1919.

Head cameraman on the picture was Milton Moore. He was assisted by Elmer Dyer, who eventually would become the dean of Hollywood aerial cinematographers. (Some of

To make Jenny appear airborne, grips rock both plane and platform as cameramen film a close-up of Ormer Locklear in *The Great Air Robbery*. Note DeMille's initials "CB" on airplane. (Cecil B. DeMille Trust)

Ormer Locklear and actress Viola Dana "ham it up" on the tail surfaces of a Curtiss JN-4D Jenny. Ormer designed the costume Viola is wearing in this gag shot. (Art Ronnie collection)

Dyer's future aviation pictures would include *Hell's Angels, The Dawn Patrol, Dirigible, Air Mail, Gallant Journey* and *Wake Island.*) Budgeted at around $250,000, the shooting schedule required less than 30 days. As soon as the picture was completed, Locklear, Short and Elliott were back on the road for another round of county fairs.

But by now a whole new cadre of wingwalkers, plane changers and stunting aerobats were getting into the act, much to the consternation of promoter Bill Pickens. Among them: "Fearless" Frank Tinney, billed as "The Aeroplane Marvel;" Eddie Conn, the "Pride of New Orleans;" George Doan in Canada, and the "Bill Staley Premier Liberty Fliers."

There were others, including a number destined to make names for themselves in other segments of aviation—Lawrence Sperry of gyroscope fame, who toured the country with an entire stable of wingwalkers; Bert Acosta, who later flew with polar explorer Richard E. Byrd; Roger Q. Williams, also to earn distinction flying the Atlantic; Maurice "Loop the Loop" Murphy, who once looped an airplane all the way from San Francisco to Los Angeles; and Lt. Roscoe Turner, yet to be elevated to the rank of "colonel" and subsequently a *Hell's Angels* pilot, prior to his winning greater honors as a champion air racer.

In Hollywood there were Frank Clarke and Al Wilson (the latter Cecil B. DeMille's flight instructor) and two or three dozen more.

Clarke and Wilson, incidentally, were both destined to become legends in the aerial movie business.

Locklear had already made up his mind to quit risking his neck in the sky, it was merely a question of when. Resembling a young Clark Gable, ears and all, he had all the attributes of a budding screen star. He had acquitted himself well as the hero of *The Great Air Robbery;* even the persuasive Bill Pickens couldn't convince Lock he'd never get barnstorming out of his blood. "Once a daredevil, always a daredevil," Pickens kept telling Locklear.

Returning from the exhibition tour in April 1920, Lock signed a contract with the William Fox Studio to star in another picture, *The Skywayman,* the story of a Lafayette Escadrille ace who had lost his memory in com-

Veteran film pilot Hank Coffin and aerialist Jimmy Goodwin execute a tricky plane-to-train transfer, for many years the hallmark of Hollywood stuntman Bobby Rose. Ormer Locklear did a similar stunt for *The Skywayman.* (Don Dwiggins collection)

Hearst International Newsreel cameraman William M. Blackwell filmed many Ormer Locklear performances, including Ormer's fatal crash, August 2, 1920. (*Los Angeles Examiner*)

bat. Through a series of daring adventures, the amnestic pilot's girl friend, played by Louise Lovely, finally "shocks" his memory back.

Curiously, the script didn't call for a single plane change, but almost every page spelled out some other type of breathtaking stunt, including a Curtiss Jenny crashing into the steeple of a church where a band of robbers had hidden. Locklear, accompanied by Milton Elliott, successfully performed the feat on their second pass. Pieces of the specially designed breakaway steeple peppered the Jenny like shrapnel, but caused only slight damage to the plane's top wing.

Although the scenario was devoid of any plane changing, one scene did have Lock dropping by rope ladder to the top of a speeding train, knocking out the villains, then climbing back up and flying off. As he had done so often before, Ormer executed the gag perfectly.

On August 2, 1920, Ormer Locklear prepared for his final scene. He had promised that this picture would be the most daring ever filmed, though constant haggling with the production people over certain technical details frustrated Ormer. For example, this last scene—a spectacular night shot of Lock's Jenny spinning down in a vortex of crisscrossing searchlight beams—had already been done in miniature. Still, Ormer insisted on repeating it "for real."

Earlier Sol Wurtzel, studio superintendent, and Lewis O'Connell, first cameraman, had discussed plans to fit their cameras with red filters and shoot the night scene during the day, using a new panchromatic film which was much faster than standard orthochromatic film. They said it would be easier and safer. Locklear rejected that, too. He refused to compromise on authenticity.

Locklear had allowed them to whitewash his Jenny, however, so that it would stand out—whether they shot the sequence in the daylight or at night. At first he protested the paint would "add over 30 pounds to the plane's weight and cut down on its maneuverability." Compounding the complexities of the problem, ten magnesium flares, attached to the wings and totaling 30,000 candlepower, would be ignited by a "hot-shot" battery switch just before the plane went into its spiral and spin. The idea was to simulate a flaming crash.

At this time, Ormer appeared more depressed than ever. Ruby Graves Locklear, the Fort Worth girl he married in 1915, and Viola Dana, an attractive young actress he met shortly after landing in Hollywood in 1919, were constantly on his mind. He was in love with Viola, but largely because of his Texas Baptist upbringing he had remained wedded to his wife Ruth. It was a nagging conflict that Lock obviously could not resolve.

At 9:15 p.m. on the night of the grand finale, Locklear and Viola Dana arrived together at DeMille Field Number 2. Director James P. Hogan scolded Lock for being 15 minutes late. Skeets Elliott, all set to fly with Ormer, got into the Jenny's front seat. Before climbing into the rear cockpit, Ormer gave Viola a quick kiss; he had invited her to go along, then decided against it. Sol Wurtzel said

she had better stay behind anyway as her insurance would be voided flying under such conditions.

A large crowd had gathered to witness the stunt, including many film stars, directors and other Hollywood pilots. Among them: Richard Arlen, a rising young actor just out of the Royal Flying Corps in Canada, and his friend Leo Nomis, a newcomer in the growing cadre of film fliers. (Nomis would be killed in a 1932 plane crash while filming Paramount's *The Sky Bride,* starring Arlen; ironically, Arlen also

Harry "Tex" McLaughlin, Ormer Locklear's successor, shown hanging by his teeth (top) and his feet. Like his stunting predecessor, McLaughlin died as he lived. (U.S. Air Force)

starred in the 1941 release *Power Dive*, the last picture Hogan directed before his death.) Another interested spectator that night was Howard Hawks, a young title writer and a pilot himself.

A mechanic propped the Jenny and its raucous OX-5 engine barked to life. At 9:40 Locklear and Elliott were in the air; ten minutes later they leveled off at 3,000 feet, bathed in the brilliant white glare of five powerful arc lights. They stunted for 15 minutes at altitude, then triggered the magnesium flares, transforming the plane into a giant sparkler as it dove down to 2,000 feet. Leveling off momentarily, the Jenny started spinning toward the ground, a spin from which the fliers never recovered.

The plane slammed into an oil sump at the corner of Third and Crescent and exploded in a ball of flame, killing Locklear and Elliott. The hands on Ormer's wristwatch, a gift of the Minnesota State Agricultural Society, had stopped at exactly 10:14 p.m.

Dick Grace, who had broken his foot in a water stunt for another picture, got to the field late. He looked toward the lights just as the Jenny entered its fatal spin. Later he remembered shouting, "Bring it out! Bring it out!" He also remembered falling as he tried to run: "When I got up, the sky was covered with red. Everything for blocks around was illuminated. The ship had fallen into the sludge pool of an oil well. *Everything* was on fire—the pool, the gasoline, the ship." (Grace, also an ex-World War I pilot, had been lured to Hollywood by Locklear; "the field is wide open," Ormer wrote in one of his letters. Dick Grace would eventually become world-famous for his *intentional* crashes in films.)

Although the exact cause of the accident was never fully explained, it is believed that Locklear and Elliott were blinded by the powerful searchlights. Director Hogan had been instructed to douse all the arcs as the plane neared the ground, but apparently they remained on. A half-dozen cameramen shot the action, including William M. Blackwell of Hearst International News, who was moonlighting to make an extra $15 as an auxiliary "camera grinder" for Fox. Blackwell had filmed Locklear's first airshow in Los Angeles on November 16, 1919. Now, less than a year later, he had filmed Lock's last performance.

Viola Dana, horrified by what she had just witnessed, had to be restrained and taken home. Interviewed more than a half century later by Kevin Brownlow for the Thomas Television series *Hollywood: The Pioneers,* the actress recalled that the shock was so great her hair started falling out. "I couldn't believe what had happened . . . I don't even like to talk about it."

Unfortunately, Ormer Locklear is a virtually forgotten hero, no doubt because his barnstorming and motion picture career lasted only 16 short months—from his professional exhibition debut May 16, 1919, in Uniontown, Pennsylvania, to his fiery crash August 2, 1920, while flying the last scene of *The Skywayman* at Los Angeles. At the time of his death Ormer was making $1,650 a week at Fox, not a bad figure considering that established stars were not paid much more. Viola Dana earned $2,250 at the time, and Gloria Swanson and Richard Barthelmess were each getting $2,500. Mabel Normand got one of the top salaries—$7,800 a week.

Having several fair contracts still outstanding, Bill Pickens replaced Locklear with Harry "Tex" McLaughlin, a young stunt pilot who had never changed planes before. He also signed another flier named James Curran to replace Elliott. And he designated Shirley Short chief pilot.

But more tragedy awaited. In Syracuse, during the new trio's second appearance,

McLaughlin, clinging to a rope ladder hanging from Short's plane, passed through the propeller of Curran's Jenny. Although badly mangled, Tex grimly hung on while Short landed as slowly and softly as humanly possible in a field of tall grass. McLaughlin's injuries were too severe, however, and he died two days later. That was enough for Short. He quit the tour, vowing never to fly such stunts again.

And he didn't. In fact, in 1926 President Calvin Coolidge awarded Short the first Harmon Trophy for his outstanding record of safety while flying the airmail. Three years later Shirley began flying for the *Chicago Daily News,* one of the first papers to use aircraft for newsgathering on a large scale. Sadly, Short and a crew of three died in the crash of "The Blue Streak," a tandem-engined Bellanca, when a wing buckled as they were attempting to set a new world record for payload.

Ormer Locklear believed passionately in the future of aviation. Despite his frightening stunts, he did promote flying safety. He also pioneered many of the techniques required of precision airmanship. He saw the airplane as a tool of commerce and a vehicle for mass transportation, as well as a weapon of war. Perhaps even more important, he advocated the development of a national airport system that would accommodate the huge armadas of flying machines he envisioned.

However, because of their fearless displays in the air, the legendary barnstormers of yesteryear were to earn a reputation for recklessness and irresponsibility that almost totally eclipsed any true measure of their more constructive contributions to the science of flight. So it was with Ormer Leslie Locklear, a Texas farm boy who lived for aviation, yet thrived on feats of derring-do. He skyrocketed to unprecedented success—and he fell just as suddenly, dead at 29.

But man can ask for little more than to depart this world doing what he enjoys most.

Chapter 3
Battle Skies and Box Office

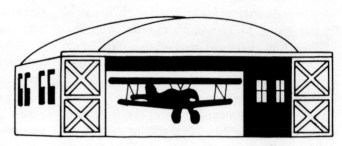

Although Hollywood didn't invent the movies, it polished and perfected them to bring the world the greatest theatrical enterprise history has ever known. Romance, adventure, laughter, thrills, fantasy—the dream factory that was Hollywood of a bygone day provided them all. From the early 1920s when the motion picture was still regarded as a mere novelty, this amazing industry matured rapidly, ultimately becoming one of the most influential and persuasive forces in modern society.

During the course of World War I, the need for escape and for news gradually overcame the old prejudices of the nickelodeon days; movie audiences representing every walk of life grew in cities and towns all across the country. As America entered the postwar decade, the people's tastes were changing, and to a certain degree, so was their screen fare.

In the "golden twenties" the gods and goddesses of the silent screen reached new pinnacles of idolatry: Douglas Fairbanks, swashbuckling adventurer; Charlie Chaplin, the great comedian; Gloria Swanson, society sophisticate; Rudolph Valentino, the great lover; and Mary Pickford, America's sweetheart. There were also the sultry Pola Negri, the "It" girl Clara Bow, and perhaps the

most famous cowboy of them all—Tom Mix.

Whether the movies shape our attitudes or our attitudes shape movies is a moot point. The fact remains that popular motion pictures are in touch with society at any given time. The great body of film can be broken down into categories, or *genres*, which in turn reflect the society and mores of their time and are closely linked with the folklore of the past. They include the western, the horror film, science fiction, comedies, crime, adventure, war, and with the introduction of sound, musicals.

But even as uniquely creative filmmaking proclaimed the birth of the American cinema as an art form, there was still a fascination with the "Great War," which didn't peak until the 1930s. It was their early portrayals of fighting fliers on the Western Front and in the battle skies over Europe that launched the careers of Richard Arlen, Gary Cooper, and a host of other stars.

For the barnstormers, motion picture flying had opened up a whole new field in aviation. Yet the number of professional fliers who actually flew for the movies is relatively small— there simply wasn't that much work to go around. While potentially lucrative, it was also a very hazardous occupation in the 1920s. Still, as movies generally gained in popularity, so

For a Fox Movietone Newsreel sequence filmed in Florida waters in the 1920s, young Mabel Cody transfers from an aquaplane to a J-1 Standard. Note cameraman in boat. Pilot Alexis B. McMullen, barely visible, waves approvingly.

Danny Grecco hangs by one hand from wing skid of a Standard J-1 during exhibition in the early 1920s. Grecco was also an accomplished pilot as well as stuntman. (Peter M. Bowers collection)

did the demand for skilled pilots.

However, not all Hollywood flying was done before the cameras, which once again underscores the mutually productive interaction between the aviation and motion picture industries. Following World War I, enterprising studio chiefs quickly adopted the airplane for sales promotion and location surveys as well as for story lines. For instance, in March 1919, pert Dorothy Dalton (who subsequently became acquainted with Ormer Locklear) flew around the country advertising Paramount Week, a studio publicity campaign. Airplanes in dozens of cities were also used to promote Locklear's first picture, *The Great Air Robbery*. So quick were movie producers to use airplanes, in fact, that film stars scarcely experienced their first plane ride before they were called upon to fly for real in a new picture, a "promo" tour, or both.

By 1921, David Wark Griffith, Associated First National Pictures, Goldwyn Film Company, Selznick Pictures Corporation, Universal Film Company, and William Fox Studios had each produced box office attractions in which flying and airplanes were an essential part of the action. May Allison, Jack Holt, Kathryn Adams, Dorothy Gish, Pat O'Malley, Jack Pickford, and Annette Kellerman were but a few of the other silent screen stars involved with aircraft in their early roles.

When the war first broke out, filmmaking had gained a very substantial place in Europe, but as the economics of war eroded the European movie industry, U.S. film producers and distributors forged ahead to a position of un-

A top performer in the Northwest, Danny Grecco poses with his rebuilt OX-5 powered Avro in 1925. Note three cockpits, ideal for carrying cameramen or passengers.

First midair refueling: Stuntman Wesley May carries gas can from Earl Daugherty's Jenny, top, to Frank Hawks' Standard in July 1921 newsreel stunt. (Security First National Bank)

disputed leadership. Now, in the wake of a devastating world conflict it was a time for heroes. Nobody realized this more than Hollywood. Moreover, the renewed interest in barnstorming, plus the prospect of breaking into American motion pictures, had already reached out across the seas.

It is said that the attractive, outgoing French pilot Charles Nungesser, who scored 45 victories in the war, may have been the one aviator most responsible for creating the image of World War I aces as handsome, hard-living rakes without a care for tomorrow. Almost totally devoid of convention, the good-looking Nungesser occasionally reported for a dawn patrol mission still dressed in a tuxedo or cutaway and accompanied by a woman. He often had to be helped into the cockpit of his plane. (After the war Nungesser's fortunes began slipping, until barnstorming beckoned. He formed a French flying circus and set out on a tour of America, recreating in 50 cities his

greatest air battles. When the circus disbanded, he went to Hollywood and starred in the 1923 silent film *The Sky Raider*. Four years later pilot Nungesser and navigator, François Coli, trying to fly the Atlantic east to west, disappeared at sea without a trace.)

Perhaps more than any other factor, however, the propagandists on both sides were the ones who deserve credit for giving us the legend of the World War I fighter pilot. Their written dispatches and pictorial releases captured the attention and imagination of the home-front reader and theatergoer who were hungry for tales of the more human aspects of an impersonal war that was otherwise beyond comprehension.

To begin with, World War I was the first war involving combat between two or more aircraft. It was only natural, then, that the cinematic legend of the aerial warrior would be born. He was America's first purely 20th century folk hero, not unlike the frontier heroes of

Charles Nungesser, who shot down 45 planes in World War I, became a model for the silver screen ace. He vanished in 1927 while trying to fly the Atlantic. (Imperial War Museum, London)

the American West. In fact, the fighting fliers took to the air with many of the mores and attitudes common to their gun-slinging counterparts who rode the range in a plethora of pulp western novels at the turn of the century.

Indeed, the American fighter pilot was a contemporary extension of the American cowboy. In the saddle on the back of a horse, or in the cockpit of a fighter plane, these American heroes were the personification of our dreams and hopes, our ideals, aspirations and values. Whether they encountered a notorious gunfighter on the loose in the west or a menacing enemy pilot in the air over France, their swift and decisive actions are qualities that strike a deeply responsive chord in American movie audiences. (Interestingly, the legend of the fighter pilot continued through World War II and the Korean conflict; the planes may have changed, but the story lines were much the same.)

By the mid-1920s it appeared the nation, and indeed the world, had grown weary of war. But two smashing box office successes, *The Big Parade* (1925) and *What Price Glory* (1926), convinced movie makers the battle theme gold mine had not yet run out.

First to sense the terrific screen potential of wartime flying material was Jesse L. Lasky, then head of the Famous Players-Lasky Company, which would soon become Paramount Pictures. John Monk Saunders, a World War I pilot and Rhodes scholar turned writer, had proposed a new film about war in the clouds. He called it *Wings*.

Lasky considered the concept: Man, the individual warrior, master of his own fate, fighting lonely sky duels above the vast, struggling mass-misery of trench warfare; helmeted, leather-clad knights of the air, in goggles and scarves, perhaps trailing a lady's silk stocking wrapped about the throat. "You can't send the boys up in those crates!" pro-tested the squadron's second-in-command. But of course someone always did. And the "boys" who survived were a new kind of hero.

Saunders was hired to adapt his own story for the screen. Another former World War I pilot, William A. Wellman, was assigned to direct *Wings*, the first truly "big budget" picture (about $2 million) in film history. Wellman (whose credits included pictures for the Fox and Goldwyn studios, among others) later recalled that he had been picked mainly because he was the only director in the motion picture business with actual combat flying experience. His salary: $250 a week.

Wellman flew in both the French (Lafayette Escadrille) and American flying corps in France. His flying buddies included Tommy Hitchcock, Jules Baylies, Dave Putnam, Reggie Sinclair, Dave Judd and Staff Brown. Returning to the States in 1918, Wellman, now a first lieutenant in the U.S. Army Air Service, taught aerial tactics at Rockwell Field, San Diego. During mock dogfights over the southern California countryside the airmen would "shoot" at each other with camera guns. (Two of Wellman's pupils in those days, incidentally, were second lieutenants by the names of Ira C. Eaker and Carl A. Spaatz. Both men rose to general rank and top command positions in World War II.) Wellman had the only French Spad in the U.S. at that time. Built by the *Société Anonyme Pour L'Aviation et ses Dérives*, the Spad (a contraction of the manufacturer's initials) was one of the most maneuverable pursuit planes to come out of the war. Consequently, Bill Wellman could fly rings around his students in their Thomas-Morse Scouts.

Lasky had already started work on the picture with another producer when he called in Lucien Hubbard. He invited Hubbard to take over the project, although Lucien never knew exactly why. Hubbard had never been a flier nor had he ever been close to fliers, but he had spent four years making big expensive westerns such as *The Vanishing American* and *Thundering Herd.*

Producers in those days didn't have the autonomy they do today. Often they were called supervisors, their primary function being to act as the official representative of the company (in this case for Famous Players-Lasky). Still, Hubbard's job was vital; he fought the "rear-guard" action against home office pressures as production costs went higher and higher. Most of the critical decisions on the picture, however, were left to Wellman's judgment.

"*Wings* was the highlight of my production career," said Hubbard, who left motion pictures to become a correspondent for *Reader's Digest* in World War II. "Nothing like it had ever been done before."

The cast included two young men who were well on the road to stardom, Charles "Buddy" Rogers and Richard Arlen. Moreover, Arlen was also an experienced pilot. The feminine lead went to the "It" girl, Clara Bow, the Marilyn Monroe of her time but one of many actresses who did not survive the advent of sound very long. Also attracting considerable attention was a tall, lanky minor player who became one of the talkies' biggest stars—Gary Cooper.

Rounding out the other principal roles were Richard Tucker, Jobyna Ralston, Hedda Hopper (later the Hollywood columnist) and El Brendel, who played the part of a German-American airplane mechanic. (What Brendel remembered most about working on *Wings* was Gary Cooper's favorite breakfast: Coke, a bowl of chili and a chocolate eclair.

More than a year in the making and released in 1927 under the aegis of Paramount, *Wings* was the last of the silent spectaculars and the first movie to win an Academy Award (for best picture of 1927/28). By the time the next date for Oscars rolled around, movies were talking. Obviously the grand sweep of air battles, the massive bombing raids and the spectacular crashes at a time when the air age was just opening up had a lot to do with the Academy's selection.

Rudimentary color—blue and red—was used in some of the flying scenes, and a recording of various sound effects and music, (but no speech) was available for theaters with the equipment to handle it.

Even today many critics hail *Wings* not only as the first important movie about aerial combat in World War I but also as the beginning of a *genre* that has not yet run its course. The plot revolves around two buddies who go into the Army Air Service together (rivals in love, comrades in the air). One is captured by the Germans and manages to steal a plane and make his escape, only to be shot down unknowingly by his pal.

Wellman and Saunders brought to *Wings* a genuine feeling for their subject—one that imitators, no matter how skillful, have never quite matched. Even today there is an awesome beauty in the aerial photography, an honest sentiment about the men who risked their lives in the challenging skies and a real horror over a giant German bomber—harbinger of the end of their kind of warfare—that is used to rain destruction indiscriminately on noncombatants.

The writer and director are equally good with the small, telling details of human behavior. In one short scene Cooper welcomes Arlen and Rogers to his tent at flight school, introduces them to the casually fatalistic attitude of the airman, quietly exits to practice "a few figure eights before dinner" and has a fatal off-stage crash, leaving them shocked, but strangely tender to pack up his belongings.

Writers Hope Loring and Louis D.

In this scene from *Wings*, Richard Arlen has just been shot down by Buddy Rogers, unaware that his best friend was escaping in a captured enemy plane. (Art Ronnie collection)

Lighton were both listed in the credits as having done the screenplay "from a story by John Monk Saunders," but scenarist Saunders did much of the scripting. Saunder's (and Wellman's) romanticized experiences on the Western Front in World War I are clearly evident throughout the film.

Lasky wangled an agreement with the War Department for the use of Kelly Field (now Kelly Air Force Base) at San Antonio, Texas, plus a gaggle of planes and pilots from the U.S. Army Air Service. From Selfridge, Brooks, Langley, and Crissy fields, as well as Kelly, came squadrons of bombers and pursuit ships—Martin MB-2s, de Havilland DH-4s, Douglas 0-2s, Curtiss P-1s, Vought VE-7s and Thomas-Morse Scouts. Scott Field near St. Louis provided balloons, officers, crews and other lighter-than-air equipment. Fort Sam Houston supplied artillery, tanks, trucks, troops and high explosives.

All told, more than 200 airplanes, including some Spads and Fokker D-VIIs brought over from Europe, were needed for the picture. About 300 pilots actually took part in it—most of them U.S. military fliers, including Henry H. "Hap" Arnold, who headed the Army Air Force in World War II, and Hoyt S. Vandenberg, who in 1948 succeeded General Spaatz as chief of staff of the now independent United States Air Force.

Professional stunt pilot Frank Tomick had charge of all the aircraft, but civilian fliers were not allowed to fly the Army planes. As a result, service pilots were assigned to each actor. For close-ups of facial expressions, the star would activate a motor-driven camera mounted directly in front of the forward cockpit, shooting toward the tail. The Army pilot in the rear seat would hunch down, giving the illusion of Rogers or Arlen flying the plane. (A tail-mounted camera also shot forward.)

The unsung heroes of aviation movies, of course, include cinematographers. Harry Perry and William Clothier were the chief cameramen on *Wings*. To put it all on film they relied mostly on the DH-4s and the larger Martin MB-2 bombers for their camera platforms; Perry made over 50 flights in the lumbering machines himself. The cameras they used were the old Eyemo, Akeley and Mitchell models.

Shooting started in the summer of 1926. Most of the exteriors were shot on location at San Antonio. The film company—actors, technicians, cameramen, pilots, and other production people—stayed at the Saint Anthony Hotel, which director Bill Wellman transformed into a movie headquarters and command post. Wellman recalled in his autobiography (*A Short Time for Insanity*, Hawthorn Books, Inc., 1974) that they were at the Saint Anthony for nine months. "I know that was the correct time because the elevator operators were girls and they all became pregnant."

Back in his flying days, Wellman's escapades earned him the nickname "Wild Bill," a descriptive name that stuck. But the biggest scene in *Wings*, a recreation of the famous battle of St. Mihiel, topped anything Bill Wellman had ever done. It involved scores of planes and pilots, some 3,500 infantrymen from Fort Sam Houston, and a specially built grandstand that was large enough to accommodate several thousand local citizens who were invited out to watch the action.

The studio arranged to use five square miles of land near old Camp Stanley. There the Army's Second Infantry Division constructed a reasonable facsimile of the "ruined" French village of St. Mihiel and its surrounding battlefield. When the work was completed, the same men reenacted the great attack on St. Mihiel. They didn't need much rehearsing—the Second had done it for real in

France eight years before. (*Authors' note:* The offensive against German-occupied St. Mihiel in September 1918 proved a tremendous victory for the First American Army—and for air power. General John J. Pershing, commander-in-chief of the Army Expeditionary Forces, credited the drive's success to the highly effective air support of Army Air Service units commanded by Colonel William "Billy" Mitchell. And characteristically, George S. Patton rode into town on the back of one of his tanks, well ahead of any other ground troops in the vicinity—a scene he repeated in World War II.)

Wellman positioned himself atop a 75-foot tower overlooking the fight. From there he could control (with push buttons) the steady barrage that preceded advancing lines of doughboys. There were 17 first cameramen and crews around the battle area's perimeter, plus 28 electrically-controlled Eyemo cameras at other strategic points.

Perched in his crow's nest, Wild Bill Wellman surveyed the vistas of the French village and the zigzagging trenches where troops were poised to go "over the top." At nearby Kelly Field, planes were warming up to take off in waves upon receiving a relayed signal. While final preparations were being made, thousands of native Texans and dozens of visiting dignitaries swarmed into the grandstand. Wellman peered over the scene one last time, then pushed the first button.

Instantly all hell broke loose. The gigantic battle scene burst into action. Artillery fired, tanks lumbered forward, and troops surged in waves over the tops of trenches. Fighting filled every corner of the Texas plain. Overhead, planes wheeled, swooped low, and barely missed rooftops as explosions erupted. Higher in the sky, individual dogfights were in progress; below, the little French village was blown to rubble.

In the midst of all the chaos Dick Grace, who would become well known for his realistic and often nearly fatal crashes, flew a Spad S. VII into the pockmarked terrain of "No Man's Land," smashing through a section of battlefield that had been especially conditioned for the crackup. He had taken off from Kelly followed by a pair of "enemy" planes (actually Curtiss P-1s), allowing himself to be shot down by the attacking "Germans" over a predesignated spot. On cue he shoved the stick forward and headed for nine square yards of marked-off, trench-dug earth.

Grace put the plane into a slight crab to the left and slammed into the ground, turning turtle as the Spad's preweakened landing gear gave way. Although a cedar log pierced the fuselage slightly aft of the cockpit less than a foot from where his head had been, Grace emerged from the bone-crushing impact shaken and bruised but otherwise unhurt. He was pleased to find that he had wrecked his plane only 17 feet away from the nearest camera.

Grace, a native of Minnesota, was a Navy flier in World War I. He had considered going into commercial aviation after the Armistice, but turned to barnstorming and jumping off buildings for a living instead. In 1920 he went to Los Angeles at the urging of Ormer Locklear. Initially he roomed with Richard Arlen, whom he first met in Wisconsin, when both were struggling for recognition in their chosen

Spad S.VII demolished by Dick Grace while filming *Wings*, William Wellman's great World War I air epic. Grace cracked up four planes for the movie. (Don Dwiggins collection)

Dick Grace, airplane crash expert and an aviation writer, lived dangerously but died in bed. At least two of his books were made into movies. (Don Dwiggins collection)

Hollywood fields.

Now Grace was crashing planes for *Wings*, a picture in which his good friend Arlen had a starring role. A firm believer in the calculated risk, Dick planned his stunts meticulously and took certain safety precautions. For the crash of his baby Spad, for example, he reinforced the cockpit with heavy steel tubing so it wouldn't collapse. Then he designed a special safety harness (lap and shoulder belt combination) that predated by many years the types used today by aerobatic pilots and race car drivers.

Dick performed four crashes for *Wings*, two of them in Spads, two in Fokker D-VIIs. His fourth and final crackup was almost his last—forever. The rigid tubular struts on his Fokker's landing gear failed to snap off as planned and Grace's head struck the instrument panel, breaking his neck. Miraculously he survived, though he spent the next several months in a hospital.

The release of *Wings* in August 1927 caused an instant sensation. It not only far surpassed the previous films based on wartime flying, it won the very first Academy Award ever presented for a motion picture. *Wings* even put to shame the more prodigious German movie *Richthofen*, which shattered the facts of ace Manfred von Richthofen's life. (But at least there had been genuine Fokker triplanes, DH-9s, Albatross DVs and even a lone Nieuport 17 in the film.)

All the other movies had one thing in common: They were done on a very conservative scale. Not so with *Wings*, a $2 million epic. The stupendous St. Mihiel battle scene alone cost more than $350,000, a *lot* of money in those days for one relatively brief episode.

Paramount's enormous success with *Wings* prompted studio moguls to produce a sequel titled *The Legion of the Condemned,* Gary Cooper's first starring vehicle (Fay Wray had the female lead). They picked Wild Bill Wellman to direct. Like *Wings*, the screenplay was adapted from a story by John Monk Saunders. (Interestingly, Wellman had tried to sell the very same story before starting *Wings*.) Also appearing in 1928 was the Colleen Moore-Gary Cooper film *Lilac Time*, perhaps the romantic apotheosis of the air-war cycle.

Lilac Time, on the other hand, was a much smaller undertaking than *Wings*. Only about 50 aircraft of various types and models were used in the picture. Chief pilot Dick Grace organized his fliers into a special squadron he called the "Buzzards." They included some of the best known stunt pilots of the day—Lonnie Hay, Ross Cook, Clement Phillips, E.D. Baxter, Frank Baker and Charles Stoffer.

Both Grace and Stoffer performed several

Scene from *Wings*, first Academy Award winner for best picture (1927/28). Left to right: El Brendel, Richard Arlen, Buddy Rogers, Richard Tucker. (Art Ronnie collection)

Hollywood stunt pilot Dick Grace broke his neck when he crashed this Fokker D-VII for *Wings* in 1927. Grace recovered and went on to wreck more planes for films. (Don Dwiggins collection)

Men who made *Wings* were reunited in 1968. From left: Harry Perry, cinematographer; Lucien Hubbard, producer; William Wellman, director; and Buddy Rogers and Richard Arlen, the stars. (Art Ronnie)

Gary Cooper's small role in *Wings* gave him the lead in a 1928 sequel, *The Legion of the Condemned*, with Fay Wray. Here he appears in *Task Force* in 1948. (*Frontier* magazine)

successful deliberate crashes for *Lilac Time*. One spectacular crackup saw Grace fly an OX-5-powered biplane into a grove of trees at 80 miles an hour, shearing off its wings and wrenching it upside down. Soon after the picture was finished, several of Dick's pilots were killed in separate accidents. One of them, Clement Phillips, died in a British SE-5 when his engine quit on takeoff.

Phillips was among a group of pilots hired by a tall, slender young man who had already determined that he would become the world's most famous motion picture producer. The young man—Howard Hughes by name—was also enamored with aviation, having learned to fly in 1925 at the time he made his debut as a producer with the unreleasable *Swell Hogan*. These two great loves—flying and film-making—would be intertwined throughout much of his adult life.

Hughes saw *Wings* shortly after it premiered in 1927 at the Biltmore Theater in Los Angeles. In fact, during the picture's run there he returned to see it several times, mentally noting specific details at each showing. Even at the tender age of 22, Howard Hughes was convinced he could make a better World War I picture than *Wings*.

And he set out to prove it.

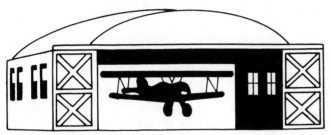

Chapter 4

Howard's Improbable Angels

In terms of its sweep, action, and budget, the air epic *Wings* was a big picture. By the same Hollywood yardstick, *Hell's Angels* was colossal!

When *Hell's Angels* was finally completed, it had cost more than $4,000,000, about double the budget for *Wings*. Over 20,000 persons had taken part in its making and more than 3,000,000 feet of film had been run through its cameras. The sheer cost of negative alone ran well over $200,000—more than the *total* production expense of the average motion picture in the 1920s.

The project also cost the lives of four pilots.

Three years in the making, the "by invitation only" world premiere of *Hell's Angels* took place May 27, 1930, at the famous Grauman's Chinese Theater in Hollywood. If *Wings* had caused a sensation, the debut of *Hell's Angels* was a blockbuster. Equally important, the movie put Howard Hughes in the big leagues of Hollywood filmmaking. (The opening night also marked the return of celebrated showman Sid Grauman, who commemorated the event by staging an elaborate musical variety program billed as "Sid Grauman's Prologue." Departing from all past tradition, the introductory entertainment featured song and dance routines in direct contrast to the theme and scenes of the movie. Grauman would also "road-show" the new picture all over the U.S. and Europe.)

Howard Robard Hughes, Jr., was born December 24, 1905. He died April 5, 1976, high over south Texas in a chartered Learjet taking him from Acapulco to the Methodist Hospital in Houston. In the intervening years Howard Hughes undoubtedly lived one of the greatest, most heroic, misunderstood, bizarre, secretive, and tragic lives in American business history.

Entrepreneur in his early years, a mysterious recluse in later life, Hughes pyramided the family Hughes Tool Company into a multibillion-dollar business empire anchored in the Summa Corporation of Las Vegas. At the time of his death, his holdings ranged from Nevada real estate and casino properties to aerospace manufacturing and airline interests. But a half-century earlier, two things occurred that, for the next 50 years, would consume much of his productive capacity: Howard Hughes became a pilot, and a movie maker.

His first venture into films was a disaster. Teaming up with Ralph Graves, an actor whom young Howard's father had once placed on the Hughes Tool Company payroll, Howard invested $100,000 in *Swell Hogan.* Graves did the rest—producing, directing, acting. The finished product was so bad it never saw the light of day.

For his next film, a sophisticated comedy called *Everybody's Acting,* he hired the successful director Marshall "Mickey" Neilan, who also happened to be an old friend of the senior Hughes. (Howard's father died in 1924, his mother, in 1922.) The movie cost $150,000 to make, but happily, it returned a modest profit. Still, nobody in Hollywood took Hughes seriously as a filmmaker except Hughes himself.

The year 1926 marked a turning point: Howard, already in control of Hughes Tool, had amended the charter of one of its subsidiaries, Caddo Rock Bit Drill Company of Louisiana, to provide a vehicle for filmmaking. He picked Noah Dietrich, a stocky, gruff-talking accountant whom Hughes had employed the year before, to oversee motion picture operations. The new enterprise would be called Caddo Productions.

Dietrich probably knew Howard Hughes better than anyone else. For 32 years he not only ran the Hughes industrial empire, but was Howard's confidante in many of his private personal adventures. In his book *Howard, the Amazing Mr. Hughes*, written with Bob Thomas and published in 1972, Dietrich recalled what Hughes once told him in a moment of candor:

"My first objective is to become the world's number one golfer. Second, the top aviator, and third I want to become the world's most famous motion picture producer. Then, I want you to make me the richest man in the world."

Hughes was 21 when he said that; to him nothing seemed impossible. Indeed, he achieved three out of his four goals. Though a superb player, golfing honors eluded him,

probably because he was too busy chasing his other dreams. He *did* set numerous world records in aviation; and he *did* amass a fortune few contemporaries ever matched. And no one who produced movies was more famous than Howard Hughes, but largely because of his fame in activities other than filmmaking. In all fairness, however, he turned out a number of solid box office hits in his lifetime.

Howard's first real winner, *Two Arabian Knights,* a clever tale about a couple of American prisoners of World War I who escape the Germans and make their way to freedom in Arabia, appeared in 1927. The silent picture cost Hughes $500,000, yet its success must be credited to director Lewis Milestone, a talented, Russian-born filmmaker signed by Hughes after Milestone broke with Warner Brothers.

For his work in directing *Two Arabian Knights,* Milestone won an Academy Award in 1928, the second year of the Oscars. The picture also made stars of its two leading men, Louis Wolheim and William Boyd, later more popular for his movie and television roles as Hopalong Cassidy.

But the idea of a movie that would glorify and perpetuate the deeds and valor of World War I fliers had been churning around in Howard's mind long before he bought his first theater ticket to *Wings* when it premiered in 1927. In fact, his director friend Mickey Neilan had even suggested an appropriate title—*Hell's Angels.* By now a crackerjack pilot himself, Hughes was more determined than ever to portray on film the exploits of Allied and German airmen.

After months of research and writing, plans were made to film an original story by Neilan and Joseph Moncure March. It was a potboiler about two World War I aces, both of whom were wooing a beautiful English society girl. This triangle would be played against a

Rare 1927 photo of Anthony Fokker, in white coveralls, who supplied Howard Hughes with Fokker D-VII fighters. Aircraft is the only Fokker XLB-2 bomber ever built.

backdrop of air warfare, including an "enemy Zeppelin" attack on London.

Ben Lyon and James Hall were cast as the two heroes. Greta Nissen, a voluptuous Norwegian, was their sweetheart. She would ultimately be replaced by an unknown—Jean Harlow.

Even as William Wellman was doing the final editing of *Wings,* Howard Hughes and a staff of aeronautical experts were rounding up all the war relics they could find. For the production's "chief of aeronautics" Hughes chose the man who had taught him to fly, J.B. Alex-

ander. Under Alexander's direction more than 80 airplanes were brought together from both sides of the Atlantic.

Anthony G. "Tony" Fokker, designer and builder of the famous models that bore his name, shipped a number of Fokker D-VIIs from Germany. Tony Fokker still had some of these aircraft in his factory in Holland; they had been smuggled out of Germany at the time of the Armistice to prevent them from being destroyed by the Allies.

To augment the enemy fleet, Hughes modified several Travel Air 3000s built in

Wichita, Kansas. This biplane in its original form, powered by the watercooled 90-horsepower Curtiss OX-5 engine, closely resembled the Fokker D-VII fighter in general proportions and especially in its use of "elephant ear" overhanging ailerons. The modified Travel Airs were soon dubbed "Wichita Fokkers."

The Allied planes gathered for the film included British SE-5s, Sopwith Camels, Sopwith Snipes, Avro 504s and other wartime types. Finally, Hughes leased a huge Sikorsky S-29 biplane belonging to Col. Roscoe Turner and rebuilt it as a reproduction of a German Gotha bomber.

Frank Clarke served as chief pilot for *Hell's Angels,* supervising more than 70 expert pilots, including some of America's foremost stunt fliers. Clarke's flight operations staff was comprised of Roscoe Turner, Frank Tomick, Roy Wilson, Earl W. "Chubby" Gordon and Harry Crandall. Clarke was also cast as

Two authentic Fokker D-VIIs used in *Hell's Angels*. Manfred von Richthofen initiated color-coding of German planes; designs were heraldic, rather than for camouflage.

Modifying Travel Airs to play the Fokker D-VIIs has been a standard Hollywood trick since *Hell's Angels*. This one (center) was Max Walton's; top, Dave Blanton's Curtiss Robin; bottom, Elton Rowley's Curtiss Jenny. (Henry M. Dittmer)

"Lieutenant von Bruen," a German flying officer. In the picture he flew a Fokker D-VII that had actually been used in Baron Manfred von Richthofen's famous *Jagdstaffel*. By the end of filming, Frank had flown the old warbird over 400 hours and had burned up five motors in the process. During one of the air sequences he also performed a spectacular 10,000-foot dive in the same ship, which indeed proved the exalted D-VII's structural integrity.

With his vast air armada mobilized for action, Hughes next leased a vast tract of land in the San Fernando Valley near Van Nuys, California. There he established an airport to be known as "Caddo Field." It became the main base of operations for the *Hell's Angels* air fleet throughout the entire production. It also served as the movie set for the allied squadrons in the picture.

Several miles up the valley near

Chatsworth, Hughes acquired another field which he built into an exact reproduction of "The Jolly Baron's Nest," a term the British had applied to Richthofen's aerodrome, the best known enemy airfield in the war.

Harry Reynolds, chief of aeronautical construction, and his ground crew of 150 men were responsible for keeping the flying machines flying. Service and repair proved an enormous task in itself as many of the war relics required the constant attention of Caddo mechanics. Hughes had a penchant for realism; he kept processed or studio shots of any air scenes to a minimum.

One of the technical advisors on the film, incidentally, was none other than Edwin C. "Ted" Parsons, who had learned to fly with Glenn Curtiss. Parsons trained pilots for Pancho Villa's revolutionary uprising in Mexico and subsequently flew and fought in the Lafayette Escadrille. An ace, he was credited with shooting down eight enemy aircraft.

Marshall "Mickey" Neilan had agreed to direct the film based on his story, but he and Hughes were soon at odds over how it should be shot. Hughes then replaced Neilan with Luther Reed, who had been the *New York Herald Tribune's* aviation editor before turning to screen writing and directing. More conflicts ensued, so Howard fired Reed and announced he would direct the movie himself.

Rumblings of the talking picture revolution were already being heard in Hollywood when actual filming of *Hell's Angels* began at the Metropolitan Studios in October 1927. Also in that same month Al Jolson's *The Jazz Singer* brought sound to movies for the first time.

At first, the film capital had treated sound as a passing fad, but not the public. The public loved talkies and demanded more, which posed a dilemma for Howard Hughes—by the end of the year virtually all the interior scenes for *Hell's Angels,* filmed *silently* at a cost of $350,000, had been completed and were "in the can."

Sopwith Snipe powered by a 230-hp Bentley was easier to fly than the Camel. Both models in the famous British series of WWI fighters were used in *Hell's Angels*.

Albatross Scouts (DIIIs/DVAs) proved formidable adversaries after Allied pilots overcame the "Fokker Scourge" in WWI, but only a very few were available for movies.

Some of the planes and pilots appearing in *Hell's Angels* pose for this publicity still in 1928. During filming, the attrition rate for men and machines was high. (Art Ronnie collection)

Six of the pilots on *Hell's Angels*, circa 1929. From left, standing: Ira Reed, Frank Clarke and Roscoe Turner. Seated: Jack Rand, Ross Cooke, and Earl W. "Chubby" Gordon.

Hughes wisely decided to scrap the footage and film it over with sound and dialogue. Obviously, Greta Nissen's thick Norwegian accent would hardly fit the image of a proper English society girl, so Howard paid her off and hired a platinum blonde named Harlean Carpenter. He also changed Harlean's name to Jean Harlow. As a result, the young actress, who had only appeared in a couple of bit parts, was destined to become the first of Howard's legendary Hollywood "discoveries."

The ten camera planes were strategically based at three locations—Caddo Field, the "German" airport close to Chatsworth, and another flying field at Inglewood, very near the site of the present Los Angeles International Airport. Frank Tomick, already a veteran of aviation movie making, supervised all the pilots who would fly the camera planes.

Harry Perry, the top cinematographer on *Wings*, was placed in charge of aerial photography, assisted by E. Burton Steene. Among the more than 25 cameramen who worked on *Hell's Angels* was Elmer Dyer, who had cut his flying teeth filming *The Great Air Robbery* with Ormer Locklear.

Bent on making his flying epic a veritable celluloid facsimile of war in the air over France, Hughes personally took to the skies in his open cockpit Waco. From this vantage point he directed the mimic dogfights, signaling instructions to cameramen and pilots by frantically waving his arms in the air.

On one occasion Hughes—with all the fervor of an authoritarian wing commander—berated his pilots for not coming close enough to camera positions on the ground. So to show what he wanted, he climbed into the nearest Thomas-Morse Scout. Immediately after takeoff he attempted a climbing right turn at an altitude of about 400 feet.

Now, any seasoned pilot knows better than to try such a maneuver in an airplane powered by a rotary engine. Just as he turned nose high, the tremendous torque of the TM's Le Rhone rotary whipped Hughes into a right-handed flat spin. In a matter of seconds the "Tommy" was a mass of crushed wood, torn fabric and tangled flying wire. Luckily, Hughes escaped with minor contusions.

During the filming high above southern California, the real-life drama that unfolded in the sky was filled with as much peril as actual combat. Time and again there were forced landings, mid-air collisions, and accidental crashes. On numerous occasions the nation's

Ben Catlin, leaning against plane, flew in *Hell's Angels*. Jimmy Robson, seated at left, was killed in this ship. Others pictured: Pancho Barnes, Bob Rath, and Wayne Merrill. (Eugene S. McKendry)

Modified Boeing P-12 sport plane built for Howard Hughes in 1929. Except for the two-cockpit configuration, this airplane was the same as Boeing's commercial Model 100. Hughes directed many scenes of *Hell's Angels* from the air, often from an open-cockpit Waco. (The Boeing Company)

newspapers told exciting stories of the daredevil pilots of *Hell's Angels* who were risking their lives to provide thrills for movie fans.

Probably the most potentially catastrophic mishap occurred when the propeller flew off Al Wilson's Fokker as he and 20 other pilots were returning to Caddo Field after "dogfighting" over the ocean near Redondo. They were flying high above a thick bank of clouds and the ground below was not clearly visible.

By the late 1920s all movie pilots were wearing parachutes, so Wilson, thinking he was somewhere over an unpopulated area of the Hollywood Hills, promptly bailed out. The abandoned, nose-heavy Fokker fell out of con-

trol, crashing in the backyard of film producer Joseph M. Schenck's palatial home on Hollywood Boulevard, not far from Grauman's Chinese Theater. The errant prop struck a sidewalk, narrowly missing several pedestrians. Wilson descended under his open parachute and landed safely on the roof of a house near the Schenck residence. But Al Wilson (no relation to pilot Roy Wilson) would figure in another accident before shooting ended, this one resulting in a fatality.

Ironically, the picture had been completed, but Hughes decided to retake a scene calling for the "destruction" of the German Gotha bomber, actually Roscoe Turner's modified 18-passenger Sikorsky S-29. Turner had used the large two-engine cabin biplane for barnstorming; he once packed 100 joyriders in the machine—all standing up—for a short hop around the field.

Earlier in the shooting schedule the big S-29 had been involved in a ground accident that nearly cost the life of cinematographer Harry Perry. Two large and expensive Mitchell cameras were set up directly in the path of the Sikorsky to catch the bomber as it was taking off. Actually, the plane was merely supposed to taxi up to the Mitchells at a relatively high speed. Barriers had been erected to restrain the bomber from lifting off. But as it lumbered down the runway heading for the cameras, the Sikorsky suddenly accelerated. It smashed right through the barriers and became airborne momentarily—landing gear and whirling propellers made metallic mincemeat out of the Mitchells, almost killing Perry when a slice of broken prop whistled by his head. The S-29 came to rest in a bean field, exten-sively damaged but repairable. It took a week to patch it up.

Now Hughes' determination to make *Hell's Angels* the most authentic and memorable action picture ever filmed set the stage for impending disaster. Although a final sequence showing the Gotha in its spinning death plunge had already been shot, Howard insisted that Turner do it again, this time with full power to make the scene even more realistic.

Turner, who had $35,000 invested in the Sikorsky and did all the "Gotha" flying himself, had spun and looped the huge plane many times, but always with power off. Even at that, he had no qualms about spinning the craft with throttles wide open, provided Hughes would pay a mechanic to check the machine from nose to tail. The S-29 had been put through a series of strenuous maneuvers; Turner wanted to make sure it was still structurally sound. Turner's request infuriated the volatile producer. Hughes wasn't so much concerned

Roscoe Turner's big Sikorsky S-29 was transformed to look like a German Gotha bomber for *Hell's Angels*. The plane crashed during filming, killing one of two crewman. (Art Ronnie collection)

about the added cost as he was the delay. To properly inspect the plane could take at least another week, possibly two.

A few days later, while Turner was away, Hughes offered Al Wilson a $1,000 bonus to put the unwieldy ship into its final spin. He then hired Phil King to ride in the mechanic's seat at the rear of the long fuselage; it was King's job to set off smoke bombs as the spinning Gotha descended, thus simulating a burning plane.

Wilson was eager to fly the Sikorsky, though most of his experience had been limited to lighter, single-engine aircraft. The fact he had never flown the S-29 didn't seem to bother him, Hughes, or even King, who stood to earn a few extra dollars himself. So Wilson and Phil King, both wearing parachutes, scrambled aboard. The engines fired and the ungainly ersatz German Gotha trundled clumsily into the wind and took off, climbing slowly.

When Wilson reached his assigned altitude, he not only changed his mind about spinning, he decided against risking a landing. For him the ship was just too heavy and unstable, so he elected to jump. He put the plane into a shallow dive and signaled King to trigger the smoke bombs, then bail out. A few moments later, Wilson himself went over the side, but apparently King never got the signal.

With its pilot gone, the cumbersome craft dove toward the earth. King, obviously unaware that no one was flying the plane, managed to ignite a couple of smoke bombs before the Sikorsky slammed into the ground and exploded, killing him instantly.

Turner tried to collect damages, unsuccessfully, claiming misuse of his property. Wilson, the man who taught Cecil B. DeMille how to fly, came in for some heavy criticism from his fellow pilots. (A few years later at the 1932 National Air Races in Cleveland, Al Wilson died in the crash of his Curtiss Pusher after colliding with Johnny Miller's Pitcairn Autogyro during a novelty exhibition.)

Although the toll of life and property was high, Hughes never gave a thought to halting production at any time. In fact, three other airmen had already been killed before King's death.

Clement Phillips, who had worked in *Wings* and *Lilac Time,* took off in his SE-5 for an air sequence when his engine began missing badly. He dropped the nose and just barely made it back to the field. After tightening a loose ignition wire, he was airborne once more, climbing steeply and banking at a dangerously low altitude. Suddenly and without warning the engine quit again. This time Phillips lost all flying speed and crashed. He died of a broken neck.

Al Johnson was also fatally injured in a takeoff accident. Departing from Grand Central Airport in Glendale for the short hop over to Inglewood, he hit some high tension lines bordering the field. Horribly burned in the wreck, Johnson was rushed to the hospital. His first visitor was Hughes.

"If he was shaken by the man's accident, Howard didn't show it," Noah Detrich recalled. "He offered a few words of comfort, but he was phlegmatic, as he was about everything. The pilot died about 18 hours after the crash."

Hughes was determined to make *Hell's Angels* unequalled for its pictorial beauty as well as for its historic authenticity. So he moved his entire company of pilots, mechanics, cameramen and technicians north to the Oakland airport. He wanted to film his expansive climactic scene over the San Francisco Bay region where there would be greater prospects for a background of billowy white clouds. But the relocation exercise proved costly in more ways than one.

To begin with, one of the pilots ferrying a

Wreckage of Stuart Murphy's Sopwith Camel after colliding with Ira Reed's Fokker D-VII while filming *Hell's Angels*. Murphy bailed out; Reed landed his crippled plane.

Sopwith Snipe from Caddo Field to Oakland ran out of gas and landed in an open field. After refueling he took off, but failed to clear a line of trees. The impact ripped the airplane apart, killing the pilot.

Next there were more mishaps during the weeks of rehearsal for what promised to be the picture's most spectacular aerial sequence—a grinding free-for-all air battle involving some 50 planes. (This would include Roscoe Turner's S-29, doubling as the Gotha bomber; it survived the initial filming, its loss occurring during a retake.)

Even though the attrition rate had been high, Hughes and his associates were able to replenish the depleting fleet with additional planes—Sopwiths, Nieuports, Spads, Fokkers, de Havillands, anything they could scrounge and make flyable. It was a test of endurance as much as skill; the script called for 22 minutes of intense "dogfighting" between the British squadron in the story and Richtho-

fen's Flying Circus.

Pictorially, the last scene would be the combat of combats. Even in practice, the noise and excitement were breathtaking. Planes brushed wings, but miraculously, there was only one serious accident.

Picture the action: diving, zooming, twisting, turning airplanes filling the sky in every direction. In the midst of the melee, pilot Ira Reed, flying a Fokker D-VII at 5,000 feet, "shoots down" an Allied plane and looks for another. Just as he spots his quarry, Stuart Murphy, piloting a Sopwith Camel, dives down from above, passing the Fokker ever so closely. Pulling up, Murphy wheels toward the Fokker and fires another burst. *Very* close . . .

Next the pilots circle back and go at it again. Murphy, a bit higher than Reed, makes another dive; this time he's *too* close! The planes collide, lock wings briefly, then separate. Murphy's lower left wing is crumpled. Unable to maintain control, he parachutes to safety. Moments later the Sopwith strikes the ground and is reduced to matchwood.

Meanwhile, Reed, stunned by the collision, surveys the damage and debates whether he should jump. Both right wings are almost torn off, the right aileron disabled completely. Shredded strips of fabric flutter in the slipstream. Reed suddenly decides he will make a desperate effort to save the plane.

Controlling the Fokker with one aileron gone is extremely difficult, but he manages it. Reed puts the plane into a shallow dive and, as he nears the ground, raises the nose slightly, then cuts the Mercedes engine. Flattening his glide even more, he pancakes the crippled Fokker into a farmer's field just ahead. He bounces a couple of times and stops, his wheels nearly buried in the soft earth.

Reed was down safely, and he had saved the Fokker from total destruction. But the immediate concern of producer Hughes was how long it might take to fix the plane. The last scene was still to be shot.

Entertainer Mel Torme, consummate World War I buff, once said of *Hell's Angels* that in filming the final sequence "the single most rewarding decision was to cast actual pilots in important roles. Frank Clarke and Roy Wilson had cameras strapped to their planes both fore and aft of the cockpit. As a result, the

A Fokker D-VII, left foreground, arcs up to intercept a British SE-5 as another enemy plane plunges to earth in this process shot from the air epic *Hell's Angels*. (Don Dwiggins collection)

HOWARD HUGHES' THRILLING AIR SPECTACLE

"HELL'S ANGELS"

The FIRST MULTI-MILLION DOLLAR TALKING PICTURE

WITH

JEAN HARLOW

BEN LYON
&
JAMES HALL

DIRECTED BY HOWARD HUGHES

UNITED ARTISTS PICTURE

Poster for *Hell's Angels*.

audience rode with them, sharing the feeling of triumph as the pursuer and of danger as the pursued."

The only trick or processed photography used in the entire 50-plane dogfight was one quick intercut of two Fokkers colliding in mid-air and falling, locked in fiery embrace. This was done with models 12 feet long that had the look and feel of the genuine article.

The only other models employed in the picture were a 60-foot replica of a German dirigible and several miniatures of British planes built to scale. These came into play for a scene based on an actual wartime incident over Calais, France, when Allied fighters destroyed an enemy Zeppelin on its way to bomb London. To ensure accuracy, Hughes hired Dr. Karl Arnstein as technical advisor. Arnstein had been a top official with the Zeppelin works in Germany during the war years.

Interestingly, Hughes had considered buying a full-size airship and modifying it to resemble a Zeppelin. However, his technical experts advised against this, convincing Hughes they could get more realistic results with a large model. In fact, these special effects would become the most impressive yet seen on film.

By the time he completed the movie, Howard Hughes had indeed produced an epic of stupendous proportions. Granted, it cost $4,000,000 to make, and four men were dead. But with all that, Hughes brought to the screen the most realistic, dramatic and thrilling film ever attempted in motion picture history. Following a sneak preview, members of the now defunct Overseas Aviators Club, then a national organization of combat pilots and observers, commended Hughes for the film's "superb realism," stating it was the "most remarkable and authentic reproduction to date of war in the air."

In the final tally it was estimated that the

50 "combat" planes and 35 camera ships had flown more than 226,000 miles in mock air battles alone. Yet unbelievable as it may seem, there was only one sequence eliminated in the final cut, besides the silent interiors Howard scrapped when he converted the picture to sound.

"The premiere of *Hell's Angels* on May 27, 1930, was the gaudiest, splashiest, star-attended affair ever seen in Hollywood," wrote Mel Torme some 30 years later. "So dense was the crowd of 1,300,000 who had come to witness the spectacle of the premiere that one movie critic complained of taking one hour to travel four blocks to Grauman's Chinese Theater."

Ever the showman's showman, Sid Grauman had Hollywood Boulevard blocked off for ten blocks, streetcars detoured, and 250 searchlights dancing in the sky, picking out 30 planes flying overhead. Nearby, the Hollywood Hills were lit up with Hughes' name.

Out in front of the theater entrance Frank Clarke's "Lieutenant von Bruen" Fokker D-VII, painted all white with wavy black striping, just the reverse of its paint scheme in the film, hung suspended from heavy cables. Klieg lights blazed and flash bulbs popped as hordes of milling, wildly cheering movie fans pressed against restraining ropes, hoping to get a glimpse of their favorite stars.

And when it was all over, the select first-night audience agreed that besides being a deeply moving emotional experience, they had just witnessed a flying film that one day would rank as an all-time classic.

Chapter 5

Let's Get Organized

Pilots Ira Reed and Al Wilson had both survived frightful mishaps while filming *Hell's Angels*, and there were many other Hollywood fliers and aerial stuntmen who had also narrowly escaped death risking their lives in front of the cameras. Producers were prone to hire only the best airmen available, then pay them in peanuts.

Although most of the artists and technicians in the movie industry had already formed craft unions by 1930, there was still no legal entity for protecting the pilots. Too few studios even bothered to insure their fliers.

To a growing number of contemporary motion picture pilots who put their lives on the line every time they went up, working for peanuts seemed sheer madness. Yet these same pilots admittedly loved to fly just for the fun of it, a passion that obviously dominated their good business sense. However, the busiest of the breed now believed it was high time they organized themselves and placed certain monetary values on their individual and collective talents. To be effective, the Hollywood pilots needed clout. They found it in the Air Line Pilots Association (ALPA), a relatively new union of professional pilots employed by the nation's young and rapidly expanding commercial airline industry.

Thus on September 29, 1931, the Associated Motion Picture Pilots (AMPP) received its charter from ALPA, an affiliate of the American Federation of Labor (now the AFL-CIO). As a result, the stunt pilots became members of organized labor, including affiliation with what was then known as the Federated Motion Picture Studio Crafts, plus the California State Federation of Labor and the Los Angeles Central Labor Council.

First to welcome the new organization to the councils of motion picture studio unions were the aerial cinematographers whose own lives often depended on the skill of pilots flying the camera planes. Stated *The International Photographer* magazine for May, 1932:

"These fliers represent a highly trained group of specialists making available to the motion picture industry the knowledge gained through the making of pictures since 1917 and the skill accumulated from over 40,000 hours of flying all types of equipment."

Actually, the "40,000 hours" referred to a combined experience level of fewer than 20 pilots who happened to be the charter members of AMPP. They included Leo Nomis, Frank Clarke, Ira Reed, Al Wilson, Florence "Pancho" Barnes, E. H. Robinson, Roy Wilson, Dick Grace, Frank Tomick, Bob Blair, Howard

Frequent mishaps while filming epics in the 1920s, like the one involving David E. Thompson, above, who survived a midair collision, moved pilots to organize. (Cecil B. DeMille Trust)

Batt, Earl "Chubby" Gordon, Oliver Le Boutillier, Garland Lincoln, Jack Rand, Clinton Herberger, Dick Renaldi, and Tave Wilson.

Objectives of the new Associated Motion Picture Pilots were fundamental: maintain the high standards of film flying, establish a base wage scale commensurate with the risks involved, and minimize wherever possible the hazards inherent in the profession. While the salutation inscribed on the charter member's AMPP certificate was more ethereal, it also projected a basic tenet of most all aviation filmmaking:

"By such association [the member] has contributed to the pictorial history of aeronautical development and left for posterity a replica of aviation achievements and progress for the pleasure and enlightenment of the world."

It's hard to pinpoint just where or exactly when the idea of a movie pilots' union was hatched. Conceivably it might have evolved at the San Marino home of Florence "Pancho" Barnes, a wealthy California socialite who turned to flying for kicks and soon became a legend in her own time. She threw the best parties in town; few of Pancho's pilot friends missed her exclusive receptions—affairs attended also by some of the all-time greats of the film colony.

Pancho got her nickname during one of her wild escapades in Mexico in the 1920s. (She first went to Mexico after a brief marriage to the Reverend C. Rankin Barnes, pastor of the Pasadena Episcopal Church.) Born July 29, 1901, and christened Florence Leontine Lowe, Pancho came by her interest in flying naturally. Her paternal grandfather was the noted balloonist Thaddeus S. C. Lowe, a man of vision who commanded the Union Army's observation balloons in the Civil War.

"He was the pioneer of today's military aviation," Pancho once said. "And if it weren't for him, the South would have won the war!"

After returning from her last adventure in Mexico, Pancho learned to fly in 1928. Her deep-seated independent streak had already led her to the movie industry; she had been an actress, stuntwoman, animal trainer, script girl, and an actress' double. Now she wanted to fly for the movies—but more for the fun of it than the money.

Yet it shocked Pancho to find out how little the fliers were paid. A wing-walker might make $25 for a plane change; crashing a ship into splinters might be worth $100. Suffice it to say AMPP had been born of necessity. In his biography of the late Paul Mantz, *Hollywood*

Pilot (Doubleday 1967), author Don Dwiggins writes:

"Before it [AMPP] came into existence, studios hired their stunt pilots from the ranks of visiting barnstormers who hung around the old Venice Field, near Santa Monica. They adhered to a rate scale set up a decade earlier by a group of fearless newsreel stuntmen who called themselves the Thirteen Black Cats."

The "Cats" got started in 1924 more by accident than by design. Ronald "Bon" MacDougall, a partner in the Burdette Airport and School of Aviation on the outskirts of Los Angeles, and two free-lance pilots, Ken "Fronty" Nichols and William E. "Spider" Matlock, agreed to fill in for some stunt fliers who had failed to show up for a scheduled air meet.

Linco Flying Aces of 1930s starred in seven movies, 27 newsreels. From left: Bill Sweet, James Taylor, Arthur De Bolt, Gordon Mougey, Joe Mackey, Myron Hightower, Edward Leach. (Bill Sweet)

Al Wilson taught flying, piloted planes for films and pioneered many intricate stunts. Here he performs an early plane-to-car change from a Jenny's wing skid. (Art Ronnie collection)

(One of the absentees was Dick Grace.) Bon flew the plane while Nichols and Matlock did the wing walking.

The threesome stayed together for five years, adding ten more members and occasionally an "honorary member" for special stunts, such as actor Reginald Denny, who had been a World War I combat pilot.

MacDougall said later that the group's original goal was to corner the market for all movie and newsreel stunt work that used airplanes, cars, motorcycles and boats. They adopted for their emblem the same spitting black cat with arched back and a full moon shining over its shoulder that Bon had been

using on his own airplane. He said it was taken from the Egyptian religion honoring the sacred cat of the Bubastisites.

When one of the fliers mentioned the superstition about Judas being the thirteenth member present at the Last Supper, it was decided to limit the group to 13. Also, the original Cats took some liberties and signed their names with 13 letters each, which helped publicize a daredevil image. Eventually the membership was expanded beyond 13.

MacDougall's partners in the airport operation, Burdette D. Fuller and Jack Frye, were first to join the original three Cats. (Frye went on to become president of Aero Corporation of California and three airline companies, including Trans World Airlines. He also served as chairman of the board of Ansco Film Corporation and of Dyestuffs, Inc.) Like the others, Frye and Fuller had been doing free-lance stunts and some barnstorming. They were also teaching flying at $20 an hour.

Another addition to the Black Cats was Jerry Tabnac, head of Cross Aerial Photo Service and one of the top aviation cameramen of the day. Then came Herd McClellan, who specialized in delayed parachute jumps; Paul Richter, Jr. (later general manager of TWA); Ivan "Bugs" Unger, who danced with his sister on the top of balloons, and Al Johnson.

Other members included Sanford "Sam"

Greenwald, one of the first ashore at Normandy in World War II and a chief cameraman for CBS-TV; Arthur C. "Art" Goebel, winner of the Dole air race to Hawaii in 1927; Bill Stapp, another International Newsreel cameraman, and Gladys Ingle, a daring stunt girl who in the 1920s completed over 300 air-to-air plane transfers without a parachute. She had many close brushes with death, but quit before her luck ran out.

There were also William "Wild Billy" Lind, who became president of an air conditioning firm in Fort Worth, Texas, and Frank Lockhart, winner of the 1926 Indianapolis 500 who died the following year in a crash at Daytona Beach trying for a new world speed record

Florence "Pancho" Barnes, one of the first women air racers and a founding member of the Associated Motion Picture Pilots, with her Travel Air Mystery S. She died in 1975. (Eugene S. McKendry) .

Ramon Novarro, second from left, star of *The Flying Fleet*, was a close friend of Pancho Barnes, left. Center, Ben Catlin, her flight instructor in 1928. (Eugene S. McKendry)

In the mid-1920s a group of pilots calling themselves the "Thirteen Black Cats" tried to corner the market for movie stunts. They had a fixed price for every trick. (Don Dwiggins collection)

Art Goebel moves his Curtiss Jenny in for the pickup as Gladys Ingle, a member of the Thirteen Black Cats, gets set up for the impending plane-to-plane change. (Peter M. Bowers collection)

Miss Ingle grabs the strut of the top plane and completes the transfer. Unfortunately, the intrepid cameraman who took these fine pictures was not identified. (Peter M. Bowers collection)

Motion picture pilot Art Goebel, who in 1927 won the Dole air race to Hawaii, with actress and ardent aviatrix Natalie Kingston, star of *Lost at the Front*. (Art Ronnie collection)

in a Stutz Bearcat. Other Black Cats who died as they lived: Matlock, who had survived two plane crashes and had ridden with Billy Arnold when he won the Indianapolis 500, was killed racing at the old Ascot Speedway in Los Angeles. McClellan invented a bulletproof vest and wore it for public demonstrations. After too many "live" tests, the vest became weakened. One day a pistol shot pierced it, killing him instantly. Al Johnson was killed in a Hall-Scott Standard while working in *Hell's Angels*.

In 1924 and '25 the Cats sent promotional circulars to every major Hollywood studio. They advertised themselves as "the world's greatest stuntmen—the only fliers who will do anything at a fixed price."

Their price list differed considerably from the union scale of today's professional stuntmen. For example, a delayed opening parachute jump with a free fall of 1,000 feet before pulling the ripcord was a standard at $150. The same fee could buy a man changing from a moving train, car, boat or motorcycle to a plane (or reverse). Some other typical charges: simple plane transfer, $100; simple parachute jump, $80; plain upside-down flying, $100; a fight on upper wing and one man knocked off, $225; a double parachute jump with two men on one chute, $180; a plane-to-plane transfer while flying inverted, $500; loop with a man standing on each wing, $450, and a spinning plane (on fire), $50.

The big bucks were in the big thrills. It

cost $1,200 to crash a plane into a tree, house or other obstruction. For the same price a Cat would spin a plane into the ground. But blowing a plane up in mid-air, with the pilot bailing out, commanded top dollar—$1,500.

At those prices, even when the stunt involved crashing and possibly demolishing a plane, the Black Cats furnished all the equipment, including the camera ship. The planes used for the crash stunts were old clunkers that could barely get off the ground. About the only thing not supplied by the Cats were the trains. Needless to say, business was good. When movie work slackened, there was always barnstorming or participating in some local air show or airport dedication.

Curiously, none of the Cats became charter members of the Associated Motion Picture Pilots. In fact, by the time AMPP got its charter in 1931 most of Bon MacDougall's original band of 13 brothers—assuming they had not already been killed—had gone on to other pursuits.

Also by then, most film fliers were trying to avoid being characterized as bold, defiant, flamboyant adventurers with little regard for life or limb. Because of hair-raising flying displays, they had gained a reputation for irresponsible daring that almost totally eclipsed their more constructive contributions to aviation.

It was the sign of a maturing industry. The

Wing-walkers Gladys Ingle, foreground, and Ivan Unger brace for another plane change. Pathé News photographer Joe Johnston cranks camera from the plane in background. (Ivan Unger collection)

Dean of "aerial housebreakers" of the 1930s, the indestructible Frank Frakes slams through a makeshift frame building for newsreel cameramen at a Los Angeles airshow. (Don Downie)

veterans even saw a certain stigma in the appellation of "stunt" pilot, for stunting implied a fearless, "hell-bent for leather" type of flying where chance and not ability usually dictated the probable outcome. They were "precision" fliers—skilled, experienced professionals whose superior airmanship set the highest standards for the fledglings who would follow.

"We really weren't a bunch of wild, reckless daredevils out to make a fast buck with an airplane," the late Ira Reed, an AMPP founding member, once told us. "We all knew the importance of proper preparation. The more in-tricate maneuvers were first diagrammed on blackboards, then worked out with models. We were also required to know camera angles and the relative performance of every aircraft involved in a scene, including photo ships."

The late Frank G. "Jerry" Andrews, a veteran stunt pilot who flew in *Hell's Angels* and in William Wellman's 1938 production of *Men with Wings*, summed it up best. He said complacency—the "it will never happen to me" philosophy—kills more people than cancer.

"Every pilot, no matter how experienced,

must always remember that a successful flight depends upon the proper balance of the three M's—*man, machine* and *mission*," said Andrews. "If any one of these critical three factors gets out of phase, regardless of whether you are flying for the movies, the airlines, the military, or a crop-dusting outfit, the flight will fail."

Andrews started flying in 1925. In the years following World War II he became one of the federal government's leading experts on aviation safety and aircraft accident investigation. He also helped develop aviation safety programs for the military, taught aircraft safety design and engineering at the University of Southern California, and ended his active aviation career as head of the safety section of The Boeing Company's supersonic transport (SST) program.

Before he died some years ago, Andrews reflected nostalgically on his motion picture flying. He recalled with amusement one incident that made a shambles of his own three-M maxim. It occurred while filming *Hell's Angels* on location near Oakland in 1928.

"It appeared flying would be cancelled that day because of rain and low ceilings," related Jerry. "So all the pilots repaired to the backroom of our favorite Italian restaurant, where we proceeded to consume several gallons of the proprietor's private stock of a potent red wine."

Crackups like this one by Dick Grace for Paramount's *Young Eagles*, with Charles "Buddy" Rogers, required long hours of preparation, but there could be no rehearsals. (Art Ronnie collection)

What happened next takes little imagination. By mid-afternoon the weather cleared and Howard Hughes summoned the pilots for a full-scale rehearsal. And an hour later the skies over Oakland were filled with 40 drunken aviators wildly mixing it up and chasing tails in a dizzy, frenetic display of whirling mayhem. As one cameraman put it, "We should have gotton the entire rehearsal on film—no real dogfight ever matched that crazy scene!"

Frank Tomick, a senior staff pilot on *Hell's Angels*, remembered that Hughes hired fledgling pilots for $10 a day, but paid the more experienced fliers $200 a week.

"Once we organized the Associated Motion Picture Pilots, however, we set the minimum weekly wage at $350," said founder Ira Reed. "But how much you made was up to your reputation. A pilot like Frank Clarke, who was without a doubt the greatest of them all, got from $750 to $1,000 a week."

Reed, who also said Clarke "started me flying for pictures and taught me everything I know," flew in more than 40 movies, beginning with *Wings* in 1926. His last was *Command Decision*. After spending some 27 years as a Hollywood pilot, Reed established and ran a small charter aviation service in Taos, New Mexico, which he described as "tougher than flying for pictures."

Besides assuring equitable remuneration for pilots and stuntmen, AMPP adopted certain safety rules governing all types of motion picture flying services. The new rules included barring tyros from participating in the most hazardous stunts, such as intentional crashes, which the likes of Clarke and Dick Grace had developed into a highly refined science.

That hazards existed in movie flying could not have been more dramatically—or tragically—demonstrated than when Leo Nomis was killed in 1932, shortly after he became first president of the newly formed AMPP.

The accident occurred during the filming of a scene for Paramount's *Sky Bride*, a "romance of the air" starring Leo's buddy, Richard Arlen, along with Jack Oakie and Virginia Bruce. Ironically, Arlen played the role of a flying circus pilot who developed a yellow streak when he believed he was responsible for a friend's fatal crash.

"Leo had injured his back shooting an Indianapolis Speedway sequence for *The Crowd Roars*," Arlen recalled. "His back may have failed him while stunting the plane; apparently he was unable to pull out of a spin."

With Nomis dead, Frank Clarke, originally installed as vice president, was suddenly thrust into the AMPP presidency. A rugged, fun-loving, nerveless ex-cowboy, Clarke soloed in 1918 at the old Venice Field, a barley patch on the edge of Santa Monica Bay. Always supremely confident of his own abilities, Frank started hopping passengers at $10 a head on the very same day he first flew an airplane solo.

Clarke earned money for his flying lessons by hiring out as a stuntman—changing planes in the air, hanging from the landing gear, and occasionally parachuting into the ocean nearby.

His instructors were Al Wilson and "Swede" Meyerhofer. What they failed to teach Frank, he invented for himself. (Swede was killed several years later in a ground accident trying to start his cantankerous old Standard when the engine backfired; he stumbled into the spinning propeller and was sliced in two.)

For his special brand of derring-do, Frank found a ready market among the makers of two-reel thrillers. But an improbable stunt written into the script of Katherine Mac-

Los Angeles authorities scolded Frank Clarke after he flew this Curtiss Jenny off the roof of a downtown 10-story building for a scene in *Stranger Than Fiction*. (Don Dwiggins collection)

Donald's new movie *Stranger Than Fiction* brought Clarke national recognition. The scene called for flying a Canuck biplane from the top of a 10-story building, then under construction in downtown Los Angeles. Permission to hoist the plane up to the roof, which was less than 100 feet wide, had been granted only on condition the actual takeoff would be faked. The director assured authorities he intended to shoot just the setup and skyline in the background. (On September 1, 1919, Ervin E. Ballough became the first pilot to land on and take off from the roof of a

building. He landed his Curtiss Jenny on the roof of the Army Quartermaster's warehouse in Newark, New Jersey, turned it around and took off, much to the astonishment of those who witnessed it.)

As Clarke climbed into the Canuck's cockpit, the cameras began grinding away. For realism, a mechanic swung the prop and the engine fired. Suddenly and impulsively Frank opened the throttle and the old biplane sluggishly sailed out over the street, already crowded with curious onlookers. Mushing breathtakingly close to the busy pavement below, the laboring Canuck finally gained sufficient airspeed for Frank to maintain control and avert a major catastrophe.

Fortunately, alert cameramen captured the entire episode on film, which also showed Clarke flying between buildings, his wingtips nearly grazing the concrete structures on either side. It turned out to be the most exciting scene in Miss MacDonald's picture. But angry public safety officials wanted Clarke's hide.

Years later Frank victimized a whole city—Omaha, Nebraska. Participating in a three-day air meet at Omaha's municipal field, the madcap of the flying movie colony spun down behind a stand of trees bordering the airport, out of sight of the spectators. He then flew away unnoticed, skimming along the Missouri River, a scant few feet above its surface. The river's tree-studded shoreline provided a perfect blind for Clarke's deception.

Certain he had crashed, thousands of would-be rescuers rushed to the opposite side of the field, through the wood and to the river bank at the point where they believed Clarke had fallen. Yet not a trace of the trim white and gold biplane could be seen anywhere on or near the placid Missouri.

After spinning below treetop level, Frank had managed to screen himself in back of the trees until he could turn and land virtually undetected at the airport's far end. Meanwhile, a massive search was in progress; any thoughts of continuing the day's program had been abandoned. Finally one of the show officials spotted Frank and spirited him away, realizing the throngs of concerned citizens, already fearing the worst, would be furious at the hoax. He was right. After learning what happened, the air show sponsors—and the city fathers—threatened to jail Clarke and throw the key away, possibly into the river.

It was at Venice in the early 1920s that Frank got his reputation for horseplay. Venice served as home base for most of the pioneer motion picture pilots, mainly because of its close proximity to Hollywood, the nation's film capital and west coast center for the newsreel industry. Clarke's insistence on the meticulous preflight planning of every aerial stunt was matched by his penchant for bizarre practical jokes.

Frank loved pets. His pride and joy was a rattlesnake named Pedro and it had the run of Clarke's airplane. Friends knew the reptile had been defanged, but strangers found it more than a little unnerving to meet a three-foot rattler some 3,000 feet in the air. (Clarke's Pedro may have inspired the snake-in-cockpit scene in Lucasfilms' 1981 blockbuster *Raiders of the Lost Ark*.)

Few of Frank Clarke's peers would dispute that he was the best. He created a number of intricate and spectacular stunts for both aviation movies and public flying exhibitions, including the so-called "whipstall" landing, a dangerously tricky maneuver only a handful of pilots have ever attempted. And despite his mischievous pranks off screen, Clarke's leadership and example in AMPP activities were largely responsible for bringing about the highest standards of professionalism in motion picture flying.

Regrettably, Frank's outrageous sense of humor proved his nemesis. On Friday, June 13, 1948, he decided to pay a surprise visit to an old friend—Frank Tomick, then operating a small gold mine in the community of Lake Isabella on the Kern River in California. Tomick purchased the mine during Hollywood's boom years of flying and returned there to live after World War II. (Too old for combat, he ferried bombers in the war.)

Clarke prepared his two-place Vultee BT-13 Valiant for the flight to Lake Isabella. As an extra surprise, he loaded a sack of cow manure in the back seat, intending to dump it out in a rolling maneuver over Tomick's mine. When Tomick heard a plane diving at his mine, he realized it could only be Clarke. But as the Valiant went into a slow roll, Tomick was horrified to see it suddenly crash and explode, killing Clarke and his passenger, Mark Owen. Accident investigators later concluded that the manure bag had shifted, jamming the controls before Owen could throw it out.

Tomick was stunned; he couldn't believe what he had just witnessed. He thought of all the narrow escapes he and Clarke had experienced together in more than 200 films. A native of Austria, Tomick had come to America with his parents in 1910. He was working as a mining engineer when World War I broke out. Always wanting to fly, he finally got his chance as a member of the 14th Aero Squadron at Rockwell Field in San Diego.

Although he never went overseas, Tomick was happy in the Army Air Service until he met Clarke in 1920, a chance meeting that would change the whole course of his life. He soon resigned from the military and became a motion picture pilot, and for many years after, Tomick and Clarke were an inseparable team. Now Clarke was dead, "killed by a lousy sack of crap."

Frank Tomick was so shaken by Clarke's accident that he never flew for hire again. In the last 20 years of his own active life he had also worked as a sound recorder, mostly at the MGM studios. Tomick died in 1966 at the Motion Picture Country Home in Los Angeles after a long illness. He was 69.

About the time AMPP came into being, Dick Grace, a charter member and the new organization's most prolific wrecker of airplanes, wrote a story about motion picture stunt flying called *Lost Squadron*. It told of gambling with death in the sky—and losing. Most of the material was a cannibalization of Dick's own experiences, however.

"I wrote it when I was depressed, when I found myself surrounded by a host of new flying faces," said Grace, "Four years before I'd organized a squadron for *Lilac Time*. There were seven regular—and one relief—pilots in it; yet at the time I wrote the story there were but two of that squadron still alive, excluding myself."

Depression notwithstanding, Dick Grace sold *Lost Squadron* to the movies. Released in 1932, Dick's story was soon followed by another picture on the same subject—*Lucky Devils*, a tale of ex-combat pilots who go to Hollywood after the war as flying stuntmen. *Lucky Devils* even repeated the overworked war film bit that saw the squadron commander erase from the blackboard the names of fallen pilots.

But not all the deadly perils of film flying were found in the skies. During the filming of First National Vitaphone's *The Dawn Patrol* in 1930, starring Richard Barthelmess and Douglas Fairbanks, Jr., pilot Earl H. "Robbie" Robinson was supposed to dive on an enemy airfield, bomb the parked "German" planes and strafe some fleeing troops. Here's what actually happened:

Technicians first hid high explosives (dynamite) in, under and around the target area. Next, a length of wire led from the powder charges to a multiple detonator operated by a property man positioned off camera. (He was substituting for the real explosives expert.) His job was to push the plunger and blow the enemy planes to pieces *after* Robbie had dropped his dummy bombs and had flown out of range. The timing was close, yet considered safe.

Frank Tomick, incidentally, also figured in this exciting tableau. Playing a German pilot trying to take off to fight the attackers, Tomick was to leap clear of his taxiing plane seconds before planted charges blew it up. The first charge would be detonated just after Robinson, following a lead plane piloted by Leo Nomis, flew past overhead.

Engines roaring and wires screaming, Nomis and Robinson, each flying a Travel Air Speedwing painted to resemble British pursuit ships and equipped with dummy machine guns,

dove down at the field. As Nomis sped by, the trigger-happy property man set off the first blast seconds too soon. Tomick jumped behind nearby sandbags barely in time, but for Robbie it was too late—he flew smack into the core of the burst!

The force of the explosion blew Robinson another several hundred feet higher into the

Douglas Fairbanks, Jr. and Richard Barthelmess in Howard Hawks' *Dawn Patrol* (1930). Picture was remade in 1938 with Errol Flynn and David Niven. (*Frontier* magazine)

Poster for Howard Hawk's *Dawn Patrol*.

air. Bits and pieces of debris from the parked airplane ripped through Robbie's wings and fuselage like shrapnel, shattering the tail surfaces and piercing other parts of the Travel Air. Cursing bitterly, he somehow managed to land the crippled plane, cartwheeling crazily as a wingtip dug into the ground. Dazed and bruised by the concussion, Robbie crawled out from under the wreck, still cursing.

Told that cameramen had filmed every spine-chilling second of his close brush with death, Robinson smiled. But when the picture was finally released, critics branded the sequence a fake! (Starring Errol Flynn and David Niven, the 1938 remake of the original picture contained the same scenes. Warner Brothers saved the expense of filming the dangerous—and costly—flying sequences by lifting them bodily from the 1930 version. For obvious reasons, the reissue of stunt footage to "stock shot" rental libraries serving the studios was one of the unfair practices AMPP union chiefs sought to stop.)

Sometimes in movie flying, consideration for the other fellow rose beyond pure friendship and became downright heroism. This was the case when Garland Lincoln, Ivan Unger, Fred Hall and Frank Austin went aloft for a scene in the late 1920s.

Lincoln was flying the ship. Unger was assisting him and had charge of releasing some lampblack to produce the effect of smoke. Hall and Austin were to bail out. (The screenplay called for the plane to have only two men in it, but the complexities of the stunt required four airmen to pull it off.) Following their jumps, Lincoln was to slow roll the plane, thus simulating the start of a crash.

Hall jumped clear and Austin followed, but the latter's ripcord hooked on a door handle, spilling his parachute inside the plane's cabin. The canopy caught the slipstream and billowed through the fuselage, knocking the lampblack out of Unger's hand. The sooty powder filled the cabin, blinding Unger and Garland.

Unger and Lincoln both wore parachutes and could have leaped to safety. But with a life at stake, the blinded Lincoln stayed at the controls while Unger pulled Austin back into the plane after an exhausting struggle that lasted several minutes. Garland, still half-blinded, finally got the ship down in a narrow canyon, stopping just short of a towering cliff.

Daring deeds like these have characterized the fine tradition of the affinity airmen hold for their fellow airmen—a willingness to risk one's own life to save another. It is an affinity woven in the fabric of many cultures, but nowhere is it more prevalent than in flying.

Also a charter member of AMPP, Garland Lincoln learned to fly in the Army Air Service in 1918. The following year he joined the Wilson Aviation Company, working with Al Wilson, C.B. DeMille and Ralph Newcomb. He left to go barnstorming in 1921, shortly after the small firm reorganized as Mercury Aviation. Lincoln subsequently operated an airfield, flew for the movies, ran a commercial aviation service and built airplanes of his own design.

At one time Lincoln owned about a dozen Nieuport 28 pursuit planes of World War I vintage. All were used in various motion pictures, including *Hell's Angels*. When the old warbirds finally wore out or were destroyed,

Lincoln designed and built the LF-1 series, popularly known as the "Garland Lincolns." They had the lines of a Nieuport and often doubled for the French fighter plane.

Garland's last picture, *Captain of the Clouds* for Warner Brothers, was filmed in Canada. Recalled to active duty in World War II, he trained pilots, ferried bombers, and flew general staff officers in the U.S. and overseas. He separated from service in 1946 with the rank of lieutenant colonel.

Besides their broad flying experience, members of AMPP had specialized skills. Each was an expert in one or more phases of motion picture flying: Garland Lincoln built planes, Dick Grace wrecked them, Frank Tomick

Donald Crisp and Errol Flynn, foreground, exchange words in 1938 remake of *The Dawn Patrol*. Edmund Goulding directed the second movie for Warner Brothers.

1938 version of *The Dawn Patrol* starred Errol Flynn. The original picture of 1930 won writer John Monk Saunders, who also wrote *Wings*, an Academy Award for best original story.

Nieuport 28, pursuit aircraft of WWI vintage. This photo, taken in 1961, also shows famed stunt and airshow pilot Cliff Winters performing a spectacular "pull-off drop" at Chino, California. (Curry & Staff)

Nieuport 17, a combat classic, was one of the best fighters of the First World War, entering service in 1916. Garland Lincoln designed and built several LF-1s, which resembled the French fighter and often doubled for it in films.

World War I ace Paul Muni discovers his gunner dead, as well as a personal note telling him of *The Woman I Love*, a movie released by RKO Radio Pictures in 1937. (*Frontier* magazine)

Frank Clarke, left, and Paul Mantz were rivals in movie flying, but respected each others' abilities in the air. They set high standards for aviation filmmaking. (Don Dwiggins collection)

always performed flawlessly, whether stunting for the cameras or flying the photo ship—and Frank Clarke, of course, a superlative flier who could fly rings around them all.

Few organizations were ever as closely knit as the Associated Motion Picture Pilots. It was as exclusive as any centuries-old London club. Yet following its founding in 1931, some other fliers eventually qualified for membership—among them Herb White, Clarence Bragunier, Jerry Phillips, Tex Rankin and Paul Mantz.

Paul Mantz probably flew continuously for the movies longer than any other pilot. But in the beginning he had a tough time joining AMPP; the group denied him membership until he had some picture credits. It was a paradox, for without a union card it was virtually impossible to work in pictures. In other words, when Mantz decided to invade Hollywood, he found himself going up against a tightly closed shop.

And that's when he also found an ally in AMPP's treasurer, the legendary Florence Lowe "Pancho" Barnes. She would make sure Paul Mantz got his chance.

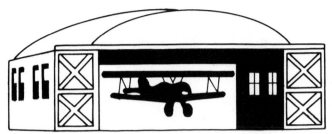

Chapter 6

Paul Mantz— Master Airman

On June 6, 1928, one day before graduation, Albert Paul Mantz was washed out of Army flying school for buzzing a train. He went on from there to become Hollywood's ace of aces, earning more than $10 million in the process, most of which he put back into aviation. But his fabulous career of movie flying that spanned some 35 years ended almost as brashly and abruptly as it had started. He simply could not resist the challenge of *one more job* before retiring. And it killed him.

Film producer-director William A. Wellman called Mantz "the best pilot in the business." To the motion picture industry, Paul Mantz was Mister Aviation. To his flying peers, he was a pilot's pilot. And though untimely and tragic, his death at the controls of a jerry-built airplane one hot summer day in 1965 was not totally unexpected.

Mantz was born August 2, 1903 in Alameda, California, just three blocks from where Jimmy Doolittle grew up. (In later years the two fliers would become fast friends.) He took his first flying lesson in 1919 on his 16th birthday. Eight years later, in November 1927, he entered Army aviation cadet training at March Field, California. He was an excellent student, standing high on the list of honor cadets.

But with one hour of solo flying to complete on the last day before graduation, Paul impulsively dove his Consolidated PT-1 trainer at an oncoming locomotive, then slow rolled frighteningly low over the nearby railroad station, sending the waiting passengers diving for cover. When he returned to his base, a hastily convened disciplinary board threw the book at Mantz and summarily discharged him. Paul's instructor, Jim Dawson, was mad as hell, but offered some sage advice. "There's a big future in commercial aviation," said Dawson. "Just learn to control yourself and you'll do fine."

Mantz did just that. He not only became dean of the movie fliers, he won fame as a film director (Cinerama), a speed pilot (a three-time winner of the Bendix transcontinental air race) and as Hollywood's favorite charter operator (his internationally known "Honeymoon Express" flew scores of film personalities to places out of state where they could get married or divorced).

He also served as a technical advisor to the motion picture industry and to other pilots, among them his good friend Amelia Earhart. He helped plan her flight around the world in a Lockheed 12, which he also helped modify. After she cracked up on her first attempt,

Mantz repaired the Lockheed and watched "A.E." try again. This time (1937) the popular aviatrix disappeared over the Pacific, a mystery that still lingers. A sentimentalist as well as realist, Mantz never quite got over A.E.'s loss; he always felt that somehow it might have been prevented. He also served as official observer to Howard Hughes' 1935 H-1 landplane speed record.

In later years, Paul delighted in telling people how the military once kicked him out, only to have General Henry H. "Hap" Arnold, chief of the Army Air Force, commission him a major in World War II. (He was later promoted to lieutenant colonel.) Not only that, Arnold gave him the Hal Roach Studios ("Fort Roach") and a supporting cast of many famous actors, including Clark Gable. His mission: Produce expert aerial photographers and a wide range of topnotch air service training films. [*Editor's note:* Another member of the "Fort Roach" team was a young lieutenant named Ronald W. Reagan. He would later be promoted to Commander-In-Chief.]

In 1929 and '30 Mantz taught flying and sold airplanes, Consolidated Fleets, first at Alameda, then at Palo Alto. One of his associates, Thomas P. Penfield, had flown in *Hell's Angels*, but no longer seemed interested in movie flying, even though he regaled in wild tales of his experiences working for Howard Hughes.

Mantz wanted to fly for motion pictures in the worst way. But he soon realized that he was an outsider, an unknown quantity. To make some newspaper headlines, while he was running a flying school at Stanford University in Palo Alto, he took a Fleet demonstrator aloft and set a world's record for consecutive outside loops—46 in all. The feat earned him national attention, but that was not enough. Frustrated, he knew he had to crack the union barrier—the Associated Motion Picture Pilots.

Paul determined he would learn all he could about Hollywood flying—the men, the planes, the studios. He soon discovered the first movie stunt pilot had been Commodore J. Stuart Blackton, founder of the old Vitagraph Studios in Brooklyn, New York.

It was Blackton who, with Albert E. Smith, had filmed the charge up San Juan Hill in 1898 (and subsequently faked the newsreel shots of the battle of Santiago Bay by filming miniature ships bobbing in a New York bathtub). Around 1910, when movies were in their infancy, Blackton found it cheaper to learn how to fly and do his own stunting than to hire a professional exhibition pilot who might command as much as $1,000 or more a performance. For pioneering the use of airplanes in films, Blackton received a life membership in the prestigious Aero Club of America, now the National Aeronautic Association.

Paul also learned that in 1915 another early movie mogul, Thomas H. Ince, used stunt pilots to add a little zest to his bathing beauty quickies produced at Inceville, his seaside studio at Pacific Palisades.

Mantz got to know the likes of Frank Clarke, Dick Grace and Roscoe Turner. Eventually he met Pancho Barnes, a charter member of AMPP (like Clarke and Grace) and the organization's first treasurer. Pancho counseled Mantz to be patient, hinting that he'd get his chance. Pancho, one of the first women stunt pilots and air racers, had already earned the respect of her fellow pilots and had been accepted in the "club."

In 1929 the bold, brusque, and brilliant Pancho won a 100-mile closed course air race for women, the first of its kind ever held. The same year she also survived a crash landing at Pecos, Texas, during America's first transcontinental air race for women, the original "Powder Puff Derby." Then in 1930 she set a new world speed record for women, flying her famous Travel Air Mystery S (for "Ship") low wing

This Travel Air Mystery S flown by Jimmy Doolittle for Shell in the early 1930s was the same type Pancho Barnes flew to create engine noise for the *Hell's Angels* soundtrack. (Beech Aircraft)

monoplane 197 miles per hour over a measured course. She broke the previous mark established by Amelia Earhart by a wide margin.

Earlier, Pancho flew the same airplane for Howard Hughes to generate engine noises for *Hell's Angels*, the first ever recorded on a movie sound track. (Sound added a thrilling new dimension to battle scenes.) Her desire to fly for motion pictures may have been inspired by her first instructor, Ben Catlin, who had flown many of the combat sequences in *Hell's Angels*.

Pancho Barnes was one of the most colorful personalities in aviation as well as in the motion picture industry. She is perhaps best known for her "Happy Bottom Riding Club," a ranch she owned near Edwards Air Force Base in California. The ranch provided a place of rest and recreation (R and R) for the test pilots of Edwards and anyone else who flew airplanes or made movies or who just wanted to indulge in some harmless fun and games.

Eventually the military declared the ranch "off limits" and in the early 1950s initiated condemnation proceedings, ostensibly because Edwards needed Pancho's land for a runway extension. Although the government didn't actually say so, it inferred that a house of prostitution was operating adjacent to the Air Force Base. Pancho herself said the pretty girls who worked for her really were cowhands, bikinis and all, and what they did on their own time was their business.

Acting as her own counsel, Pancho sued the Air Force, claiming, among other things, that she had been defamed. Unfortunately, during the course of litigation, the clubhouse and all its trappings burned to the ground. It was believed to have been arson.

In any case, after a series of sensational court fights, Pancho was awarded a $414,000 judgment. She may have been the only woman in history to sue the United States government and win.

But the story of this remarkable woman

doesn't end there. It is true that the military tried to banish Pancho from her own land. Yet, it's also true that the great big federal government had a change of heart with respect to Pancho Barnes and her role in the scheme of things, including, we must assume, her contributions toward improving the quality of life around Edwards. In November 1980 no less a personage than Secretary of the Air Force Hans Mark stepped forth to officially dedicate a new "Pancho Barnes Room" at the base officers club.

The room is impressively decorated with memorabilia and photographs relating to the history of Edwards and its famous test pilots, among them Chuck Yeager, Pete Everest, Joe Walker and Neil Armstrong.

Pancho would have been proud. Sadly, she'll never see it. She died in 1975. And there's another tragic footnote to her story. Six weeks before the dedication ceremonies at Edwards, Pancho's only son, Bill Barnes, was killed when the P-51 Mustang he was piloting crashed in the California desert on the way to a fly-in. At the time of the accident, Bill was in the process of restoring his mother's old Travel Air Mystery S. (As this is written, plans for a film based on Tom Wolfe's 1979 best seller, *The Right Stuff*, may include the reconstruction of Pancho's Happy Bottom Riding Club. As one Hollywood observer said, "It could be one helluva movie!")

By 1932, Hollywood filmmakers had recognized the AMPP as the only accredited organization in town whose members were true masters of their trade, duly qualified and superbly able to fly any craft from a small single-engine "flivver" to a huge multiengine trans-

Florence Lowe "Pancho" Barnes in the cockpit of her Travel Air Mystery S, circa 1930. Her paternal grandfather was the noted pioneer balloonist of Civil War fame Thaddeus S.C. Lowe. (Eugene S. McKendry)

94

When Pancho Barnes married Eugene McKendry in 1953, General Albert Boyd, then commander of Edwards AFB, and renowned test pilot Chuck Yeager were official witnesses. Over 1500 attended. (Eugene S. McKendry)

port or bomber. Moreover, the AMPP pilot would fly it with machine-like precision through almost any type of aerial maneuver or scenario an imaginative script writer might dream up.

True, there were so-called "wildcats" in the business who would try to fly a powered barn door for a buck. Often these "fly-by-nighters" tried to undercut the AMPP fee and salary rate scale, but Mantz soon found that most major studios were now looking more for quality and reliability than pure economy.

Mantz also learned that his skill as a pilot would not be his only requirement. He would have to know cameras and camera angles and be able to work in harmony with his director in obtaining effective shots. And he might be called upon to contribute authentic slang for a screenplay or take his turn as technical director to rule inflexibly on dialogue and the dress of characters and the suitability of props and other equipment. Part of the job, he learned, might involve finding appropriate locations for his picture.

Paul had the basic credentials. He held an unlimited commercial pilot's license issued by the aeronautics branch of the Department of Commerce (now FAA—the Federal Aviation

Pancho Barnes' much publicized ranch near Edwards AFB was often used for movie making. Left to right: Jackie Ridley, Jimmy Doolittle, Jr., Chuck Yeager, Shelly Winters, Dave Schilling, Pete Everest. (Eugene S. McKendry)

Administration). Equally important, he was eligible to receive from Commerce a certificate of waiver permitting low flying, stunting, the operation of unlicensed aircraft and various other deliberate infractions of air law, provided other lives and property were not endangered.

But as he made the rounds of studios, without an AMPP card Mantz couldn't get past the casting offices. Convinced he faced a no-win situation, Paul again consulted Pancho. The wonder woman of Hollywood lit a cigar, put her arm around Mantz and said, "Paul, there's some work around here the boys won't touch. Find it."

Mantz did. He found a job none of the other pilots had bid on—a $100 stunt for a scene in *The Galloping Ghost*, a movie based on the life story of football hero Red Grange. The gag seemed easy enough; all it required was to fly low past a ground camera with a stuntman on the top wing. And, of course, it also required an AMPP card. So once again Paul applied for membership. This time Frank Clarke, who had succeeded Leo Nomis as president upon the latter's death, told Mantz the dues were $100.

Paul was furious. The dues *had* been $10. Now it would cost exactly what the lousy job paid. However, the wise and astute Pancho saw through Clarke's strategy immediately and urged Mantz to pay up. She even offered to loan him the money. "It's the best deal you'll ever get," said Pancho.

Thus after weeks and months of frustration and disappointment, Paul Mantz finally gained access to the sanctity of motion picture flying, an exclusive fraternity of airmen as well as a Hollywood trade union whose roster of star male pilots included but one notable exception—Florence "Pancho" Barnes. Mantz was proud indeed to have at last won the confidence of his fellow airmen. Although the animosity between Paul and Frank Clarke was

still there, it would fade in time. And it certainly never altered the fact that each man shared a mutual respect for the other's abilities.

Mantz also found out why the other pilots had rejected *The Galloping Ghost* assignment. According to the script, he was supposed to fly a Stearman biplane through a Hollywood Hills canyon, where a camera crew waited, while an agile young stuntman named Bobby Rose made like a monkey, scampering all over the top wing. Flashing down between canyon walls, Mantz suddenly saw a tall sycamore looming dead ahead. He tried banking around it, but nothing happened. He had lost all lateral control. Rose's cavorting antics had blanketed out the ailerons.

It was the kind of emergency Paul hadn't even anticipated, one that demanded instant reflex and the right decision. Mantz quickly shoved the stick forward and dove toward the ground, hauling back just as the wheels struck the canyon floor. The plane bounced up through the top branches of the tree and came to rest on the other side, somewhat the worse for wear. Rose landed in a heap, suffering abrasions but no broken bones. Pancho Barnes complimented Paul for his cool head and correct action. "You are one of us now," she said. (Interestingly, Bobby Rose, who started out as a jockey, then doubled for a number of stars and even wrote film scripts for Ruth Roland, would work with Mantz in many pictures, including *The Flight of the Phoenix*, which claimed Paul's life in 1965.)

So well did the AMPP pilots perform, they had a virtual monopoly on motion picture flying. Besides stunt flying, studio chiefs relied on them for technical advice, piloting camera planes and directing aerial sequences. In fact, the pilots became as familiar with the industry's problems in making movies as they were with their own operational problems. As

Veteran movie stuntman Bobby Rose flew with Paul Mantz on Paul's first picture, and—some 35 years later—his last. Rose survived countless mishaps. (Don Dwiggins collection)

Flexibility and performance of Paul Mantz's Lockheed Sirius made it ideally suited as a camera platform. He used it extensively for motion picture work in the 1930s. (Al Bachmann)

a result, Hollywood's major studios often gave the AMPP fliers full responsibility for developing and executing aviation sequences.

Paul Mantz saw a growing potential for motion picture flying, even in the lean depression years of the 1930s. He set out to win the respect, trust and goodwill of the entire motion picture industry. He organized United Air Services, Limited, and became the first tenant on United Airport in Burbank, a new field established by United Air Lines.

An entrepreneur and innovator, Mantz had put together the nucleus of an operation that in future years would evolve into Paul Mantz Air Services and, eventually, Tallmantz Aviation (the latter including, as an adjunct, the now widely heralded "Movieland of the Air"). But for starters, Paul's United Air Services owned three airplanes—his Fleet demonstrator, a three-place Stearman camera ship and a red and white Travel Air stunt plane. He also rented storage space in his leased hangar,

although he let Pancho Barnes park her Travel Air Mystery S there free in exchange for the use of it on a split-fee basis.

Business was good and getting better. Lockheed Aircraft moved to Burbank and a number of Lockheed customers soon stored their own airplanes with Paul. This in effect expanded the size of the Mantz fleet, for Paul would arrange for the use of virtually all the planes he hangared.

His first big picture, *Air Mail* for Warner Brothers, not only proved his mettle, it brought him the plaudits of a usually blase film colony. All Mantz had to do for one major scene was fly his Stearman through the Bishop (California) Airport hangar, a space only 45 feet wide when the doors were open. But Bishop's location compounded the problem. It lay at the foot of the mighty Sierra Nevada range, at the head of Owens Valley, where chilly, gusty winds often rushed down the slope to blend with scorching thermals in the desert furnace. The resulting mixture formed violent whirlpools and eddies of unpredictable turbulence.

The picture's chief cameraman, Elmer Dyer, already well on his way to becoming Hollywood's top aviation cinematographer, mounted a camera on Paul's plane. Dyer very honestly had some reservations when he heard Paul Mantz, a relatively unknown, had been signed for the shot. But when he saw Mantz fly, Dyer's fears quickly vanished.

Mantz flew the scene flawlessly, but not without its moments of stark terror. He literally fought to control the bucking Stearman as the deadly Sierra wave, a cold stream of Pacific polar air, tumbled down the eastern escarpment of the range, slapping at his plane with sledgehammer blows. And to make matters worse, blustery hot winds sent billowy clouds of sand churning across the airport, at times virtually obscuring the field from Paul's vision.

Air Mail marked the start of a whole series of flying through hangar doors, a stunt that almost became Paul's hallmark. But in the life of this remarkable man, it was only the beginning.

For *Blaze of Noon*, based on Ernest K. Gann's best-selling novel about the early air-

Paul Mantz spins earthward for *Air Mail*, trailing smoke. Director John Ford is seated on ladder. Elmer Dyer, right atop truck, and a second cameraman capture the action on film. (Elmer Dyer)

100

Flying through hangars became a standard stunt after Paul Mantz negotiated the first one for *Air Mail* at Bishop, Cal. Feat is not as easy as it may appear. (Tallmantz Aviation collection)

mail days, he spun an airplane down to ground level—and then some. For *When Willie Comes Marching Home* and *Suzy* he flew old biplanes between two trees, shearing off all four wings in the process. For *Twelve O'Clock High*, a 20th Century-Fox release and 1949 Academy Award nominee for best picture, he piloted a "crippled" Boeing B-17 Flying Fortress solo, landing it wheels up on its belly precisely where director Henry King had prescribed.

In addition to his work in front of the cameras, Mantz continued to perform flying exhibitions in some of the country's biggest air shows, notably the annual National Air Races. In fact, during the early 1930s Paul Mantz, Frank Clarke and Howard Batt flew together as the "Hollywood Trio," one of America's first non-military aerobatic demonstration teams. Show announcers played up the rivalry between Mantz and Clarke, especially during their "head-on" passes.

Mantz piloted a red and white Boeing P-12; Clarke, a white and gold Stearman, and

Batt, a blue and red Travel Air. They specialized in tight formation flying. Hugging each other so closely that wings overlapped, the daring fliers put their planes through every heart-stopping maneuver in the book, accentuating each dazzling figure with trailing colored smoke. In one spine-chilling stunt Mantz flew upside down in "wheels-to-wheels" formation with Clarke. In another, he and Clarke raced toward each other on a terrifying collision course, where the slightest miscalculation could mean death. At the very last instant the planes would bank away sharply and pass, barely missing one another.

Other pilots who substituted for one or more members of the Trio included John H. "Jack" Rand and Easton Noble. Batt and Rand also flew in *Hell's Angels* and were charter members of AMPP.

Paul's exuberance was boundless, matched only by his great sense of humor. Flying back to location one day for *The Bride Came C.O.D.*, starring Bette Davis and James

Cagney, he rolled his P-12 and made a roaring low-level *inverted* pass over the assembled cast below. There was a light rain, and a movie cameraman on the ground told the cowhands who had been hired as "extras" that Mantz always flew on his back when it was raining—just to keep his face dry.

Over the years charter flying represented a substantial share of Paul's income. His "Honeymoon Express" became a Hollywood fixture. (His first "Express" was a Lockheed Vega.) "I took most of the stars to Yuma and later to Las Vegas to be married," Paul once told us, "and sometimes I took the same people to Las Vegas or Reno to get a divorce."

In some 30 years of charter operation, Paul or his pilots flew them all, from Jean Harlow to Lana Turner. He brought cowboy star Tom Mix's body back to Los Angeles after Mix was killed in an auto accident in Arizona.

Harold Krier in a Great Lakes, bottom, and Charlie Hillard, in an Akromaster, complete a variation of the "head-on pass" made famous by Paul Mantz and Frank Clarke.

Harold Krier in his Chipmunk, bottom, and Charlie Hillard, flying Ed Mahler's plane, recreate another thrilling Paul Mantz-Frank Clarke airshow routine of the 1930s.

(Mix was a good friend; he had flown airplanes, driven racing cars, and in 1920 had served as one of Ormer Locklear's pallbearers.) Mantz also transported the body of William Randolph Hearst from San Simeon to San Francisco. His charter customers included some of the country's largest industries, such as Ford, Lockheed and Convair. Bing Crosby and Bob Hope were among Paul's dozens of "regulars."

As an Army Air Force officer in World War II, Mantz instructed aerial photographers and produced numerous flying training films. One of his many unusual assignments was to fly a B-17 up the tricky fjords of Greenland for an instructional movie that would show ferry pilots how to maneuver into "Bluie West One" and other nightmarish fields.

In the postwar years Mantz claimed the famous Bendix race as his own. He flew a pair of modified North American P-51C Mustang fighters (numbers 46 and 60) to three successive victories: 1946, 1947 and 1948. (He had flown a Lockheed Orion to third place in both the 1938 and 1939 Bendix races.) The only three-time winner of the Bendix, Paul won more than $125,000 in prize money with "Number 46," including a $10,000 side bet from oil tycoon Glenn McCarthy who had entered a Lockheed P-38 Lightning in one of the races. (The bet was rather conclusively settled when the Lightning suffered a massive engine failure shortly after takeoff and the pilot, Jim Ruble, bailed out. McCarthy was a good loser; the next year he sponsored Mantz to the tune

of $75,000.) Mantz also used his Mustangs to publicize the movie *Blaze of Noon*. [*Editor's note:* One of the Mustangs, N1202, passed into the hands of Charles F. Blair, where, as "Excalibur III," it became the first single-engine aircraft to fly nonstop over the North Pole from Norway to Alaska. This airplane is now at the National Air and Space Museum, where it has been magnificently restored.]

Throughout his career Mantz shunned the term "stunt flying." He preferred "precision flying," and precise he was. If a movie studio asked him to handle a particularly dangerous flying job, Paul would go out and inspect the site for the shooting. Then he would carefully and meticulously plan all the intricate phases of the gag itself—measuring, calculating and computing the answers he needed to make the stunt as safe and as effective as possible.

"He was not a wild pilot," states retired

This Boeing 100 Special, civil version of Army P-12, was flown by Paul Mantz in the "Hollywood Trio," an aerobatic exhibition team that included Frank Clarke and Howard Batt. (Al Bachmann)

After Paul Mantz beat Glenn McCarthy's P-38 in the 1947 Bendix race, McCarthy decided to join the winning team and sponsored Mantz for Bendix '48. Mantz painted P-51C N1204 pearl gray and switched his favorite race number, 46, over from Mustang N1202, in which he had won the Bendix the two previous years. He won again in '48. (Leo Kohn via Joe Christy)

Air Force Lieutenant General James H. "Jimmy" Doolittle in *Hollywood Pilot*. "And while he did very spectacular flying it was all thought out beforehand. I would not say he was a daredevil, in the sense that he took unneces-sary risks. He always had the equipment, the training and the skill necessary to take most of the hazard out of flying."

But on a hot July 8, 1965, near Yuma, Arizona, in a place called Buttercup Valley, a

Paul Mantz "gently" noses over landing during a film stunt. Consolidated and Stearman biplanes were favored for stunting; both afforded good protection. (Paul Mantz collection)

No less a pilot and personage than Gen. James H. "Jimmy" Doolittle praised Paul Mantz's flying abilities. "He was not a wild pilot. He always had the equipment, the training, and the skill necessary to take most of the hazard out of flying."

long, oval hollow in the desert floor, surrounded by 60-foot sand dunes, lurked a hazard that conceivably could have been created by a prairie dog. And it would end Paul's life and seriously injure his friend, veteran stuntman Bobby Rose.

Producer-director Robert Aldrich needed some tricky flying to make movie audiences believe an unbelievable 20th Century-Fox production called *The Flight of the Phoenix*. The film featured an all-star cast headed by James Stewart, himself a veteran pilot and a brigadier general in the Air Force Reserve, with a distinguished flying record in World War II.

The picture's plot involved a transport plane (a twin-engine Fairchild C-82 Flying Boxcar) that crashes in the Sahara. Instead of waiting to die of thirst, the crew members and passengers construct a weird single engine aircraft from pieces of the wreckage. Hopefully, they name it the *Phoenix*, after the bird in Egyptian mythology that rose from its own ashes. In one wild, climactic scene, the *Phoenix* struggles into the air and flies off to civilization.

For the flying sequences, Aldrich went to Tallmantz Aviation, Inc., a company formed in 1961 when Frank Tallman and Paul Mantz joined forces. It was a natural merger, one that combined over 60 years of aviation experience, much of it gained in flying for motion pictures. The resulting organization gave two aviation movie impressarios—Frank and Paul—a good hold on the Hollywood market. (By 1965 Mantz had piled up some 25,000 hours as a pilot; he had pulled off impossible stunts in more than 250 movies. But also by this time Paul did most of his film flying behind the cameras. From his combination pilot seat and director's chair, he liked to fly the Tallmantz firm's specially-equipped B-25 camera plane, "The Smasher," best. He supervised the aerial shots for such flying films as

Strategic Air Command, Spirit of St. Louis and *The Crowded Sky*, and the Cinerama spectaculars *Seven Wonders of the World, America the Beautiful* and *Deluxe Tour*.)

Otto Timm, Paul's old friend and former associate (who designed and built his first airplane in 1911 and then taught himself to fly it), came out of retirement to help construct the hybrid *Phoenix*. (Mantz's crew scavenged some components from an old twin-engine Beech C-45 and a single-engine North American T-6 trainer.) Though purposely made to look like a rattletrap, the plane met all FAA regulations for homebuilt aircraft.

In *The Flight of the Phoenix*, survivors of a desert crash jury-rig a makeshift plane with parts of the downed aircraft. For movie filming, Tallmantz Aviation made the real article. (20th Century-Fox)

107

Paul Mantz seemed to enjoy the challenge of flying this hybrid machine, aptly named the *Phoenix*. But technical and environmental problems dogged flight operations from the start. (20th Century-Fox)

The *Phoenix* had never flown when its builders shipped it to Yuma in late June. Actually, Frank Tallman had been slated to fly it originally, but a simple accident in the driveway of his own home changed everything. Pushing his son's go-kart, he fell and shattered his left kneecap, which kept him from flying the scene. (Later infection set in and the leg had to be amputated above the knee.) Mantz wanted to fulfill the commitment, even though Fox studio executives felt that at his age—nearly 62— he was too old. When Paul heard of their

concern, he laughed and said, "I'll put on one *hell* of a show!"

Mantz found the plane nose-heavy, but flyable. The original plan called for him to take off from the floor of Buttercup Valley. He was supposed to make the *Phoenix* appear to haul itself into the air, bouncing along the desert, kicking up great clouds of sand, and then rising at the last instant to clear the dunes. But Paul argued that he could never get off in the sand, so the plans were changed. He would simulate a takeoff by flying into the valley, dipping down

108

Paul Mantz tries first of two hybrid aircraft specially built for *Flight of the Phoenix*; stuntman Bobby Rose is in rear seat. Mantz was killed in the other flying article. (20th Century-Fox)

until his wheels touched the surface (the wheels were mounted in landing skids) and then pulling up to hurdle the dunes.

There are no buttercups in Buttercup Valley. There *are* rattlesnakes, and at one time the area was also populated by a burrowing rodent commonly known as the prairie dog. The main characteristic of Buttercup Valley is the crushing heat. It is a huge outdoor oven, making it perfect for shooting desert pictures, and Hollywood has been doing so there since Ronald Colman starred in *Beau Geste* in 1926. Because

For "just one more shot," pilot Paul Mantz begins his final run. In the following photo series taken from actual film clips, the camera records a horrifying sequence. (20th Century-Fox)

At instant the plane touches down (top), its fuselage begins to break. Center, the split widens as the *Phoenix* digs into the surface. Bottom, it starts to cartwheel. (20th Century-Fox)

Top, the *Phoenix* snaps in two as its forward body rolls over and over and smashes into the ground. The heavy engine tore from its mounting and crushed Paul Mantz. (20th Century-Fox)

temperatures often reach 130 degrees or more in the afternoons, the flying shots would be taken in the early morning, just as soon as there was sufficient daylight.

The single-engine monoplane that Tallmantz had built was, in the vernacular of a modern teenager, rather gross. Mantz and Bobby Rose sat in tandem cockpits so shallow the upper half of their bodies seemed to be sticking out in the open air. Four poles slanted out of the fuselage, converging in a single point about five feet above the pilot's head. (The rig was supposed to be a king post anchoring cables that helped hold on the wings.)

Paul prepared for his first pass on the morning of July 6, but he had to turn back when his engine overheated. The next day he was too close to the cameras.

So on July 8 at 6:10 in the morning, with Rose in the rear seat, Mantz was airborne again. Coming over the dunes at about 100 feet, he descended with power on and made a good pass. On his second sweep, Paul touched down twice and barely cleared the western dunes. It was excellent. But the directors wanted what the trade calls a "protection" shot, in case something happened to the first. For over three decades movie producers had been congratulating Mantz for his sensational flying scenes and then asking for *just one more*.

Mantz circled the dunes, then radioed he was coming in. As the *Phoenix* kept descending, Frank Pine, manning a ground control post, radioed Mantz that he was low enough.

But Paul never acknowledged the transmission. He continued down, then scraped the desert floor. Suddenly his right gear hit a small mound no more than six or eight inches

A brilliant aviation career ended abruptly in the arid Arizona desert. The tragic crash killed Paul Mantz, but Bobby Rose, though badly injured, lived to fly again. (20th Century-Fox)

high—but baked hard by a boiling sun. (The hummock might have been the work of a long ago prairie dog, Pine speculated later.) Paul gunned the Pratt and Whitney engine with a great roar, but it was no use. The plane's long, thin fuselage was already breaking in two. In another split-second the propeller dug into the parched desert, flipping the *Phoenix* over on its back as pieces somersaulted along the valley floor.

Paul Mantz died in the crash. Bobby Rose lived through it. And though cameramen filmed the fatal accident in its entirety, it never appeared in the finished picture. Just as planned, *The Flight of the Phoenix* shows an awkward, patched-together makeshift airplane fighting its way into the air, sluggishly lifting over the sand dunes rimming Buttercup Valley, and then flying off to safety. (The four "men" who appeared to be riding on the wing were actually silhouette plywood cutouts. Mantz and his associates tried dummies at first, but the dummies blanketed out the controls, much as Rose's body had done on the Stearman when filming *The Galloping Ghost* years earlier.)

Paul's last flight was not really necessary. He had already done the job on his previous tries. But he agreed to fly the scene again for one more take. And as promised, he put on "one hell of a show."

Chapter 7
Movieland of the Air

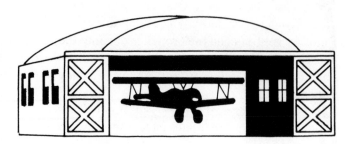

Two weeks before Paul Mantz was killed, a former flying partner, Richard "Dick" Grace, who crashed some 50 airplanes for motion pictures, succumbed in the Veterans Hospital in West Los Angeles on June 25, 1965. As fate would have it, he died not of crash injuries, but illness. Grace was 67.

Although of different temperament and persuasions, Paul Mantz and Dick Grace were cut from the same cloth. Both had lived for flying; both were perfectionists in their respective specialties. They shared an abiding common interest: aviation history. Indeed, their interest was not wholly self-serving or self-aggrandizing. These two independent men, each in his own way, wanted to preserve and perpetuate for present and future generations the great heritage of the American airman.

Dick Grace not only cracked up airplanes and did general stunt work, he wrote extensively about his experiences—books, articles, movie scripts, and at least one successful novel. For example, Dick's little-known attempt to fly a single-engine Waterhouse Cruzair monoplane from Hawaii to the United States in July, 1927 (the flight ended in a wreck on the island of Kauai) is treated in his autobiographical *Squadron of Death* and *Visibility Unlimited*.

Grace's first literary effort is believed to have been "Fall Guys," a three-part article published in the *Saturday Evening Post* in 1929. Then in the same year his book *Squadron of Death* came out, and in 1931 *I Am Still Alive*. Also in 1931 *Liberty* magazine published *The Lost Squadron* as a serial; it was made into a movie and published as a book in 1932. His *Devil's Squadron*, according to a listing in the *New York Times Directory of the Film*, appeared in 1936.

Dick may not have had the facility for writing that he did for flying and stunting, but he nevertheless made a substantial contribution to the body of aviation literature.

It has been reported that Dick Grace broke more than 80 bones performing intentional crashes for the movies. Because of his medical record, he was denied combat duty in World War II—until he managed to "arrange" an overseas assignment, despite a protesting Army surgeon general's recommendation against it. Grace completed 44 missions as a bomber pilot over Europe, flying B-17s and B-24s. He returned from one raid on Germany with a piece of flak in his thigh.

Paul Mantz was not a man of letters, but a man of dreams. Like most creative, imaginative people, he had a passionate urge toward

Actor Fred MacMurray at the controls of his Spad VII in 1938 Paramount release *Men With Wings*, a film in which Paul Mantz and Tex Rankin did much of the flying. (*Frontier* magazine)

excellence in anything he undertook. Frank Pine, an ex-Navy flier and another longtime associate, described Paul as a "goer and a doer."

Mantz had long harbored a desire to build an aviation museum. In fact, his idea for collecting and displaying classic aircraft in an educational motif might well have been sparked in 1938 while filming William Well-man's Paramount movie *Men With Wings*, a romantic history of aviation starring Ray Milland, Fred MacMurray, Andy Devine, Kitty Kelly, and Louise Campbell. The story line traces the development of aviation from the time of the Wright brothers to the production of America's most advanced (for their day) multiengine bombers.

"The country should have some 'living'

A faked shot for *Men With Wings*: The Spad in foreground was a studio prop hung by wires, while the "Wichita Fokker" behind it was projected on a screen. (Frank Stranad collection)

More hokum, but an effective illusion, again from *Men With Wings* of 1938. Here a "Wichita Fokker" doubles for the German fighter. Note dual smoke pipes mounted under its fuselage. (*Frontier* magazine)

Fokker in this studio process shot was actually a Travel Air built in Wichita, Kansas. Specially posed scene from *Men With Wings* shows Spad VII in hot pursuit of the enemy. (*Frontier* magazine)

record of those grand old planes," Mantz said some 25 years ago. "Those old crates are symbols of the period in which the seeds of today's aviation industry were planted."

After the war he bought 500 surplus airplanes for $55,000 and became sole owner of the "seventh largest air force in the world," ranking right ahead of China. (It was also something for the United Nations to think about, his owning nearly 100 B-17s, over 200 B-24 Liberators, more than a score of twin-engine bombers and exactly 137 fighters.) Incidentally, he got his money back immediately because no one realized the airplanes still contained plenty of aviation gasoline in their fuel tanks—almost 500,000 gallons.

It was inevitable that Paul Mantz and a young man named Frank G. Tallman III would combine their talents. What started out as a friendly rivalry for lucrative film contracts ended up as one of the most viable and unique collaborations in the field of aviation services—or show business.

Frank Tallman's romance with airplanes began at an early age. Born to a prominent midwestern family in 1919, he logged his first flying time sitting on his father's lap. His dad, a former Navy pilot, had bought a two-place open cockpit biplane when Frank the third was only eight. From that moment on, young Frank yearned for the day when he could share the same sky with his youthful idols—Eddie Rickenbacker, Frank Luke, and Raoul Lufbery.

Tallman attended prep school in Connecticut but graduated into airplanes, soloing in 1938. During World War II he served as a naval flight instructor at Pensacola, managing to check himself out in every type of aircraft in the Navy inventory.

Following the war, Tallman worked as an advertising account executive with the Columbia Broadcasting System (CBS), flying in air shows on the side. A man of vision (like Paul Mantz), Frank Gifford Tallman also nurtured hopes of some day building an aviation museum. His love of vintage aircraft, in fact, first bloomed in 1949 when he spotted the skeleton of an old Sopwith Camel, a 1917 British fighter, tucked away in an old barn near Moorestown, New Jersey. Only an experienced eye would recognize the tattered remains as a rare bird. Tallman located the owner, who sold him the Camel, plus five other World War I relics—a Spad, Fokker D-VII,

DH-4, Nieuport 28 and a Thomas-Morse Scout. Total price: $500.

Frank spent $3,500 putting the Camel into flying shape. Considered by some the greatest fighter of the First World War and credited with destroying 1,294 enemy aircraft, the Camel had tricky handling characteristics due to the aerodynamics of its short fuselage and stubby wings with high dihedral in the lower planes, and its rotary engine—either a Clerget or Bentley—that revolved around a fixed shaft, producing tremendous torque. Flying it could be a harrowing experience, but Tallman mastered the little beast on his first flight.

Leaving the world of advertising for a career in aviation, Tallman toured Europe looking for more antique planes. He had already sampled a taste of Hollywood flying dur-

Fred MacMurray wins the French *Croix de Guerre* in Paramount's *Men With Wings*. He won the same medal again as Eddie Rickenbacker in Fox's 1945 *Captain Eddie*. (*Frontier* magazine)

During an exciting career, Frank Gifford Tallman III, who was equally at home in a hot air balloon or high performance jet, flew some 500 different types of aircraft. (Tallmantz Aviation)

ing his Navy days (he retired from the Naval Reserve as a lieutenant commander in 1956). For Frank Tallman, performing aerobatics in front of the cameras held a special appeal. Thus he decided to specialize in movie stunt flying and authentic classic aircraft. So he continued searching the world's "attics" and found many other incredible treasures, including a 1909 Blériot.

Tallman returned in time to fly in Bill Wellman's *Lafayette Escadrille,* the air epic featuring Tab Hunter, David Janssen, Clint Eastwood and William A. Wellman, Jr. (Warner Brothers released the picture in 1958.) By now Frank was stunt flying in earnest. He had also moved to California with his priceless array of vintage civil and military aircraft. Initially he operated out of Riverside's Flabob airport.

Soon the name Frank Tallman began appearing on more and more screen credits, especially the *Bob Cummings Show*, a popular television series in which Frank flew an old biplane and Bob's own Beechcraft Super 18. (Cummings, a pilot, owned the "18" for several years, occasionally leasing it to Howard Hughes.)

By this time Frank Tallman and Paul

Pilot Bob Cummings, with author Jim Greenwood, was a flight instructor during World War II. His popular TV series *The Bob Cummings Show* often made use of airplanes. (James Yarnell)

Frank Pine preflights Tallmantz Aviation's B-25, a converted bomber that has probably filmed more Hollywood air epics since World War II than any other fixed-wing aircraft. (Bob Serpan)

Mantz were spending a lot of energy—and money—competing for movie work. Realizing they had much to gain by uniting, they got together on the Jimmy Stewart movie *The Spirit of St. Louis*, building and flying a reproduction of the Ryan monoplane Charles Lindbergh flew across the Atlantic in 1927. It marked their first major collaboration. Then in 1961 they officially merged their interests into a single corporate entity—*Tallmantz Aviation.*

Tallmantz, a composite of their last names, combined two growing collections of aircraft, including Paul's specially modified

B-25 camera planes and his favorite P-51 racer (he had since disposed of his enormous military fleet). But the new partners "didn't want just a bunch of dusty airplanes sitting around." They were determined to put each antique in its true background, relating each item to its proper time and period.

In July 1963, at Orange County Airport in Santa Ana, California (now John Wayne Airport), Charles "Chuck" Yeager, the first man to fly supersonic, had the honor of breaking ground (with a gold-plated shovel, no less) for the construction of a new air museum, a dream

Paul and Frank each had cherished privately for many years. Today this *Movieland of the Air* museum houses may of the glamorous relics the two men accumulated during long associations with motion picture flying. It includes a wide variety of historic aircraft, engines, armament, artifacts and other memorabilia spanning the history of flight—from balloons to jets. (All museum exhibits are available to film studios, advertising agencies and television; in fact, most of the airplanes on display are still flown for the movies and TV.)

Meanwhile, Frank Tallman continued to prove his skill and resourcefulness in scores of films (he was also a charter operator, cropduster and experimental test pilot). For Stanley Kramer's movie *It's a Mad, Mad, Mad, Mad World* in 1962, Tallman buzzed a control tower far inside safety margins, taxied an airplane through a glass wall of an airport restaurant, and flew a twin-engine Beechcraft through an open hangar.

But the "stunt of stunts" saw Frank fly the Beech through an outdoor advertising billboard, a gag that required weeks of preparation and practice. A dummy sign of cloth and tapes was set up in an Orange County pasture and Frank flew through it repeatedly, until he felt comfortable with his "approach" to target.

The movie billboard on location was constructed of balsa wood and styrofoam, held in place by a heavy steel frame embedded in con-

In a scene reminiscent of the old plane-auto contests of an earlier generation, Frank Tallman matches his Curtiss Pusher against a vintage racer at Ontario, Cal. (Don Dwiggins collection)

Port view of B-25 camera ship *Lively Lady* shows photographer Liz Clark in nose. Plane pioneered the "Circarama" film system, an outgrowth of wartime "Vitarama" gunnery trainer. (Bob Serpan)

crete, much like the basic structure for a permanent building. Because there wasn't much ahead of the cockpit to absorb the shock, Tallman and Paul Mantz, who would be directing the flight sequence, reinforced the Beechcraft's nose and windscreen. Adding to the risk, of course, was the alarming fact that the plane's wingspan left less than three feet of clearance on each side.

Tallman aimed the nose of his plane dead center of a yellow circle on the back side of the billboard (out of camera range) and smashed through at 160 miles an hour, scattering debris in all directions. And as he had correctly pre-

dicted, he lost 50 percent of his available power—the right engine, stuffed with pieces of balsa wood and styrofoam, went dead. Moreover, the windshield that had been so carefully beefed up also shattered on impact, splattering the pilot with slivers of glass and other assorted debris. Frank radioed the nearby Orange County Airport, requesting permission to make an emergency landing. The tower responded in the affirmative and he came on in without further incident.

Until he fell pushing his son's go-kart in 1965, Tallman's only serious injury was a broken ankle sustained in a sport parachute jump.

And because his infected knee prevented him from flying the *Phoenix*, he blamed himself for the death of Paul Mantz on an Arizona desert. To make matters worse, three days after Paul was buried, Tallman underwent surgery. Doctors removed the leg just above the knee, and told him he might never walk again.

For many people, the trauma of such a personal loss plus the physical incapacitation might have meant the end of a fruitful, productive life. But not for Frank Tallman. Instead, he was determined not only to walk, but to *fly*.

Fitted with an artificial limb, Frank began the grueling task of learning to walk and fly all over again. Incredibly, *one year later he had requalified for every single type of FAA airman's license that he had held before the accident*. It is believed that at the time, Tallman was one of

fewer than 20 persons in the world to hold all the pilot ratings, including jets, and the *only* amputee so rated.

A typical day at Tallmantz might find Frank flying around Orange County in a 1909 Blériot in the morning, test-hopping a 1917 French Nieuport before noon, digesting his lunch while performing aerobatics in one of the very few flyable German Pfalz fighters in existence, and then taking off in a de Havilland Vampire jet to film a TV sequence in late afternoon. And after all that, he would hop into a Cessna 310 and commute to his plush Palos Verdes home, 30 miles away.

Proving his ability to fly with the old finesse, Tallman soon landed some of the toughest movie assignments in Hollywood. And there were none tougher than *Catch-22* for

In the "stunt of stunts" for Stanley Kramer's 1962 hit *It's a Mad, Mad, Mad, Mad World*, Frank Tallman flew this twin-engine Beechcraft through an outdoor advertising billboard. (Mrs. Boots Tallman collection)

124

Even this "bulletproof" windscreen, taken from a fighter and installed in Frank Tallman's Twin Beech, shattered as the plane went crashing through the billboard at 160 mph. (Frank Pine collection)

Paramount. It presented perhaps the thorniest problems—and the greatest risks—of all. For openers, the Tallmantz organization had to put together an entire squadron of 18 B-25s, recruit the pilots and build a complete World War II air base at a remote location in Mexico. The difficulties associated with finding the planes, training the crews and providing efficient logistical support were, to say the least, staggering!

The six months Frank and his staff spent filming on location involved some of the most demanding flying any of them had ever done. Each morning before the cameras began rolling, all flight operations personnel underwent briefings as detailed and thorough as those in

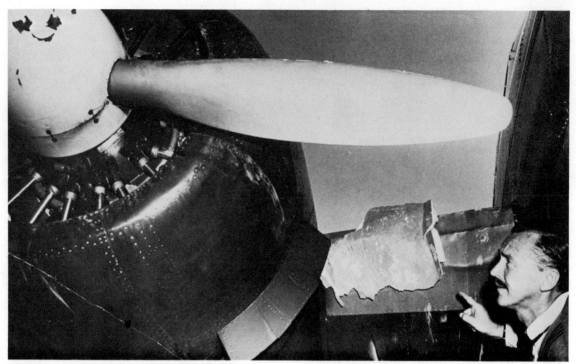

Billboard stunt was no piece of cake—sign debris killed the right engine on impact. Frank Tallman examines damage to Beech 18's cowl and wing leading edge. (Frank Pine collection)

real wartime. The way Tallman kept not only his own flying but that of his pilots up to the highest professional standards earned him the respect of cast, crew and movie industry alike.

For a sequence in *The Carpetbaggers*, Tallman had to fly inches over a parked truck and land a biplane on a narrow street. So close did he come to hitting the truck with his wingtips that cameramen shooting the scene actually ducked. For *Reward*, filmed on a Tucson river bed, he not only crashed a plane, but had to release a smoke bomb, simulating a fire, before crawling out of the wreckage.

In *Murphy's War*, a Paramount release starring Peter O'Toole, Frank piloted a single-engine Grumman J2F "Duck" amphibian biplane, a type that served the Navy in wide-ranging duties from 1934 until the early 1950s. Location for the picture was in the steaming jungle area of northern Venezuela. Landing on

the Orinoco River one day, Frank struck an unseen object in the water and felt the aircraft shudder violently as a lower wing bucked and an aileron froze. Somehow he nursed the damaged plane 60 miles back to home base. Now, spare parts for a 40-year-old airplane are not easy to come by in the Venezuelan jungles, but Frank found a former German U-boat commander who operated a small machine shop nearby. Within a few hours they had jury-rigged the necessary replacements.

A stickler for realism, during the filming of *Wake Me When It's Over* he brought his P-51 Mustang down on one wheel not once but *eight* times. He wanted to be sure that it "looked good" on film.

The Great Waldo Pepper for producer-director George Roy Hill was something else again. A story of barnstorming in the wake of World War I, it is not so much about any one

126

character (Robert Redford plays Waldo Pepper) as about the many who chased the sun from town to town in open cockpit biplanes, thrilling people in rural areas who seldom saw a flying machine of any kind. The superb aerial sequences were supervised by Tallman, who also did much of the flying. And one unintentional crash nearly cost Frank his life.

The movie, released by Universal Pictures in 1975, was based on a story by Hill, a pilot himself and the proud owner of a Waco UPF-7, which he hangars at Movieland of the Air. William Goldman, whose credits include *Butch Cassidy and the Sundance Kid*, also for George Roy Hill, wrote the screenplay.

[Editor's note: Bill Goldman researched much of his script for *Waldo Pepper* in the Greenwood home, where the authors maintain extensive archives of early aviation material, especially of the barnstorming era.]

Tallman looked like *he* should be playing the lead. He was tall, lanky and deeply tanned by many hours of flying in open cockpits. The corners of his sparkling eyes were etched in crow's feet creases, as if he were constantly squinting at the sun. He combed his light brown hair straight back over typically English features and the bristling sandy moustache he sported occasionally curled up at the ends rather roguishly. Dressed in the appropriate

Frank Tallman dives low in Joseph E. Levine's 1963 film *The Carpetbaggers*, starring George Peppard and Bob Cummings, both of whom are also pilots in real life. (Paramount Pictures)

Standard J-1 of the type used in *Ace Eli and Rodger of the Skies*, a 1973 release filmed in Kansas. Cliff Robertson starred; Frank Tallman flew the air scenes.

uniform, he could easily have been cast as a World War I fighter pilot—for *either* side.

Frank was particularly enthusiastic about *Waldo Pepper* because of the period of aviation it represented. For the more hazardous stunts and crashes, he put on a rubber mask and doubled for Redford. But the man who walked wings in the picture, and who looked like Redford, was *Redford himself*—a terror-stricken Redford, but Redford nonetheless. Other actors, like Ed Herrmann and Bo Brundin, who played "Ernst Kessler," were also exposed to some real live aerial maneuvers for purposes of authenticity. Hill wanted none of the close-ups in any of the flying scenes filmed by process photography. The character "Kessler," portrayed by Brundin, was actually patterned after Ernst Udet, a World War I German ace and well known exhibition flier who toured the U.S. in the early 1930s. Udet committed suicide in World War II.

"We were awfully lucky—no one died," said Hill. "We took the chances and we ended up with some bad crashes, not counting the intentional ones, some hospital bills, a few interesting scars, but no fatalities. I am, and always will be, enormously proud of the actors for their courage as well as their talent."

Hill also heaped praise on the professionals who did the air work, beginning with "the great Frank Tallman" and including an incredible 63-year-old wing walker, Ralph Wiggins (who wouldn't wear a parachute), and pilots Frank Pine, Jim Appleby and Art Scholl. "They flew those old airplanes within an inch of their lives," Hill stated. "I hope that some kid is making a scrapbook of them today, because by God, they really are dashing and debonair and devil-may-care and fearless."

One of Tallman's most difficult pieces of business during the filming called for a low level flight down the main street of a town *between* the buildings, just as the more daring barnstormers did in the old days. His wingtip window clearance left no margin for error.

Hill selected Elgin, Texas, for the sequence (Florida and California were other locations for flying scenes). Universal studio technicians moved power lines underground to clear the route of the flight and altered the buildings somewhat to project a 1920s atmosphere. To duplicate an actual barnstorming stunt, Tallman flew his Standard J-1 all the way through the scene with a "woman" perched on the left wing. The unpredictable wind currents at street intersections increased the risk, but Frank negotiated the episode safely.

Not so safe were the circumstances surrounding some ferry flights as a result of the producer's efforts to maintain production schedules. Asked if there had been any unplanned accidents, Hill responded:

"Not while we were on location, but we did wipe out three planes while we were shoot-

Hair-raising stunts like this car-to-plane change highlighted action in *The Great Waldo Pepper*, a 1975 film about airshow flying 50 years ago. Frank Tallman is flying the Standard J-1.

Screen star Robert Redford in his role as the great Waldo Pepper, an early barnstormer. Air sequences for the movie of that name were supervised by the late Frank Tallman. (Universal Studios)

ing on the California location. I tried to get the combat planes into our location too soon after a heavy rain and we rolled a Garland Lincoln Nieuport into a ball when it hit a soft spot in the field. Then Frank Tallman was flying a replacement Nieuport and coming in for a landing when his rudder pedal broke off and he went in through high-tension wires. It was a very bad crash and hospitalized Frank for over a month, and we had to shut down for part of that time."

Hill added that pilots in the film company also wiped out a few landing gears and a couple

World War I ace Ernst Udet, with champion woman flier Dorothy Hester in this 1931 photo, was model for German pilot featured in *The Great Waldo Pepper*.

Frank Tallman flies Standard J-1 down Main Street of Texas town in scene from *The Great Waldo Pepper*, released in 1975. Note stuntman on wing, dressed as a woman. (Universal Studios)

of wing panels. But what he didn't mention was the fact that the two most serious "unplanned" accidents both occurred on the very first day of shooting!

Fortunately Frank Pine, pilot of the Garland Lincoln, emerged from his wreck unscathed. Tallman, though badly hurt, was also lucky. However, if he hadn't hit the power lines, which helped deflect and slow his Nieuport as it spun toward the ground,

Tallman most probably would have been killed. Jim Appleby, trailing in a Tiger Moth at the time of the crash, watched Tallman's plane suddenly snap roll and spin. Appleby said the first thought that flashed through his mind was, "I don't know what the hell you're doing down there, Frank, but if you think I'm going to follow you, *you're crazy!*"

If those two incidents didn't shake producer George Roy Hill, certainly the next one

Robert Redford as Waldo Pepper struggles to free pilot of wrecked experimental plane while cameraman films action. Crash scene was meticulously planned and rehearsed. (Art Scholl)

should have unnerved him completely. Later the same day, Appleby took the Tiger Moth up with Robert Redford in the rear cockpit. Suddenly his engine quit. Jim expertly maneuvered the Moth into a successful deadstick landing, but with a movie "talent" on board, the outcome could have been catastrophic.

The "stock" planes used in *Waldo Pepper* included three de Havilland Tiger Moths, two Standard J-1s, two Curtiss JN-4D Jennies, a Fokker triplane, a French Stampe, a Sopwith Camel (built up from scratch) and the Nieuports. Also in the cast was a de Havilland Chipmunk that Tallman modified to resemble an early monoplane. To create the appearance of a vintage experimental prototype, Frank fitted motorcycle wheels and tires to the Chipmunk's landing gear and installed cabane wires

on its upper frame.

In the movie, Waldo Pepper's friend Ezra Stiles (played by Edward Hermann) designs the low wing monoplane, then crashes it attempting the world's first outside loop. Stiles becomes trapped in the wreckage, which catches fire when a spectator's cigarette ignites spilled fuel. Unable to remove his friend from the cockpit, Pepper bashes Stiles unconscious with a piece of wreckage to spare him a horrible and painful burning death.

In another episode, Pepper gets sore at finding Axel Olsson (a Swedish pilot played by Bo Svenson) working what he considers to be his turf. While the Swede isn't looking, Waldo loosens the axle nuts on his rival's Jenny so that on takeoff the wheels drop off. In the story the hapless Swede pancaked into a lake. But in

Tallmantz Aviation experts disguished this de Havilland Chipmunk to resemble an early monoplane prototype, a so-called "advanced" type of plane central to *Waldo Pepper's* story line. (Universal Studios)

real life Tallman actually "ditched" one of the expendable Tiger Moths modified to look like the Swede's Curtiss JN-4D.

For the scene showing the "sabotaged" Jenny's takeoff, the wheels were fixed to jettison by a spring arrangement on the pilot's command. In order to land the Jenny without wheels, however, brackets holding small, two-inch industrial rollers or casters, barely perceptible on film, were welded to the axle. And because the gear had literally *no* shock absorption capacity, Frank had to land the airplane *very* carefully on a smooth runway at an abandoned Air Force base nearby.

Tallman's last major assignments included work in the television series *Black Sheep Squadron* and the Warner Brothers movie *Capricorn One*, released in June 1978. *Black Sheep* was a dramatization of the exploits of Major Gregory "Pappy" Boyington's renegade bunch of Marine fighter pilots who flew in the South Pacific during World War II. *Capricorn One* was a fictional story about America's first manned space shot to Mars—a flight that turned out to be a hoax.

In *Capricorn One* the three U.S. astronauts (James Brolin, O.J. Simpson, and Sam Waterston) are plucked from their space capsule just before liftoff, whisked to a hidden sound stage in the desert, and forced to simulate TV transmissions as though they were on Mars. They escape and the *real* flying starts.

The astronauts steal a Learjet, hit a car on takeoff, thereby losing the left main landing gear, and then run out of fuel and make a belly landing in the desert. A search team in an old Stearman piloted by Telly Savalas (who plays a cropduster), with newsman Elliott Gould in the passenger seat, finds Brolin, picks him up on the wing, and leads a merry chase against two Hughes 500C turbine helicopters. (*Capricorn One* will be covered in more detail in Chapter 10.)

Frank said afterward that flying his Stearman through California's Red Rock Canyon, repeating hair-raising stunts for 40 flight hours over a three-week period, had been one of the most dangerous motion picture jobs of his long career.

Ironically, at 3:14 p.m. (PST) on April 15,

1978, just two days short of his 59th birthday, Tallman lost his life during a routine flight in his Piper Aztec. He and a client, Michael Wilson, had been in the San Francisco area that morning and the day before, scouting locations for a new James Bond film titled *Moonraker*. (Wilson was executive producer of *Moonraker*; more information on this picture is given in the next chapter.) Returning from San Francisco, Tallman dropped Wilson off at Santa Monica and refueled. Frank then departed alone for Phoenix, Arizona, where he had other business. Although the weather around Los Angeles was bad, and much worse in some other areas on his flight path, he was flying VFR (visual flight rules).

Frank failed to clear a ridge in the Cleveland National Forest (along the Santa Ana Mountains) near Trabuco Canyon, California, southeast of Los Angeles. His plane impacted at an altitude of 3,100 feet—about 400 feet below the crest. (Earlier the nearest weather station had reported 600 feet overcast, one mile visibility and heavy rain.) At the time of the crash Frank had logged more than 21,200 hours of flying in all manner of aircraft—from hot air balloons to the most advanced, sophisticated jets.

The National Transportation Safety Board (NTSB) listed the probable cause simply as "continued VFR flight into adverse weather conditions." The NTSB added, however, that among the contributing factors were unknown visibility at the accident site, an overcast, rain, and a "high altitude obstruction"—the standard accident report definition for mountainous terrain.

Tallman's death stunned the aviation community and the motion picture industry alike. Because of his experience, his skill, and above all, his demonstrated judgment, such an accident was unbelievable, if not inconceiv-

For *The Great Waldo Pepper*, Frank Tallman's crew welded tiny casters under Jenny's axle. After shooting wheel-shedding takeoff scene, Tallman landed out of camera range. (Universal Studios)

In this character study taken on location of *Black Sheep Squadron*, Frank Tallman's pensive, reflective mood projects image of every veteran airman who has "touched the face of God." (James W. Gavin)

able. In fact, Frank seemed indestructible, having executed some of the most daring flying ever staged before Hollywood cameras. Many a movie and television show owned more of its popular success to his performance than to the actors who received star billing.

Frank Tallman was a master performer and a gentleman. He brought to aviation that enviable blend of professional flying expertise and uncompromising integrity. The standards he set for the pilots who would follow remain a living tribute to his talent.

Chapter 8
Tough Acts to Follow

Frank Pine, a crusty, seasoned ex-Navy flier, wise in the ways of the motion picture industry, succeeded Frank Tallman as president of Tallmantz Aviation, and he determined to carry on in the Paul Mantz-Frank Tallman tradition. But he also recognized that flying for films had changed drastically in the years since World War II, as had movie and television production techniques.

Pine streamlined the organization, increasing its efforts in areas not subject to the cyclic needs and economic whims of filmmaking. That's *not* to say Tallmantz Aviation had given motion picture work lower priority. No, indeed. It simply means Pine is expanding those activities that generate a steadier income, such as aircraft maintenance and modification, commercial aerial photography, charter flying and the many other basic aviation services Tallmantz offered.

"We do all kinds of strange things with airplanes and to airplanes," Pine said recently. "We took a hard look at the money in movie flying and decided we wouldn't work for fame anymore. Now the shop's gross tops our film revenue."

Also, more and more pilots were getting into the act, most of them veterans of the Air Force, Army, Navy or Marines who had flown

in World War II, Korea or Vietnam. By the late 1950s, the Associated Motion Picture Pilots was little more than a memory—one of the nostalgic focal points of many Quiet Birdmen (QB) meetings in the Hollywood Roosevelt Hotel, but no longer a recognized bargaining agent for the brotherhood of airmen who fly and stunt in the movies today.

Now pilots who want to take up movie flying seriously must become members of the Screen Actors Guild (SAG), the well-known trade union (AFL/CIO) that has jurisdiction over all performers working in feature films, television, commercial spots and, in many cases, even in industrial movies. A number of the more active fliers in Hollywood, especially those spreading their wings in directorial fields, also belong to the Directors Guild of America, formerly known as the Screen Directors Guild.

To join the Screen Actors Guild (as of this writing), it costs an initiation fee of $500, plus semiannual dues of $25. But as one example of the benefits (and there are many, such as pension, insurance, etc.), SAG membership assures pilots of earning the going scale for salaries and wages. The current minimum rate is $520 a day. Prices for hazardous stunts are negotiated. (The costs of building, leasing and

Ex-Navy commander Frank Pine at the helm of Tallmantz Aviation's B-25. He has filmed just about everything for movies, including belching volcanic eruptions of Mount St. Helens. (Jeff Marks)

operating aircraft are also handled separately.) The base daily rate when Pine started in motion pictures in 1960 was $175, which compares with AMPP's minimum charge of $50 a day for straight flying back in 1940.

A few pilots also belong to the several fraternal organizations of professional stunters. James W. "Jim" Gavin, one of the busiest pilots and second unit directors in Hollywood, is a member of the Stuntmen's Association of Motion Pictures. So were the late Frank Tallman and Howard Curtiss, the latter a pilot and skydiver best known for his role in the *Ripcord* television series. (Curtiss and another jumper were killed September 2, 1979, when they collided in free fall during parachute competitions at Lake Elsinore, California.)

Two other groups are the Hollywood Stuntmen's Association, a workshop for teaching neophyte stunters, and Stunts Unlimited, also a fraternal organization.

Hal Needham, a co-founder of Stunts Unlimited, who rose to the top of his profession, once earned $8,700 for three weeks' work on *The Spirit of St. Louis,* walking wings and performing "cutaway" jumps with five parachutes. (Needham would open one chute, release it, then open another, and so on, until he finally descended under the fifth.) Hal later turned director. Among his recent credits are two Burt Reynolds films, *Smokey and the Bandit* and *The Cannonball Run*.

Perhaps it should be noted here that stunts with parachutes are as much a part of the aviation film genre as flying machines. There is no more spectacular or dramatic cinematography than the air-to-air camera work of parachutists in free fall. The *Ripcord* TV series was a classic example. So was the 1969 movie *The Gypsy Moths,* starring Burt Lancaster and Deborah Kerr. It's the story of three barnstorming exhibition parachutists, one of whom is killed jumping a batwing rig called "The Cape." The other two then put on a show in his memory and prove that the dangerous stunt can be done.

More recently, stunt parachutists B. J. Worth, Rande Deluca, Jake Lombard and Ron Luginbill did the filming and doubling for an aerial scene in the 1979 United Artists' release *Moonraker,* featuring Roger Moore as James Bond (007) and Richard Kiel as the steel-dentured baddie named "Jaws." In the skydiving sequence, the pilot (Worth) of a hijacked aircraft bails out, leaving the passengers on their own. Then James Bond (Lombard) is thrown from the plane without a parachute. His perennial foe "Jaws" (Luginbill), wearing a parachute, follows in pursuit, even as Bond fights the pilot for his chute as all three fall through space. Bond gets the pilot's chute and the horrified pilot plummets to his "death." 007 snaps on the chute just in time for another freefalling fistfight with "Jaws." Bond terminates this altercation by pulling his ripcord. For the grand finale, "Jaws" yanks his own ripcord clear out of the chute and freefalls into a circus tent.

This exciting episode was cleverly "gaffed" by Worth and his associates. (*Gaffing* is a studio term for stunt work—it means figuring out how to do the stunt without killing anybody.) Not only did the jumper have to be *highly* proficient in conventional free fall skills, he was also required to have a good understanding of film. He had to be continually aware

James Bond fights pilot of hijacked aircraft in *Moonraker*, a 1979 release. For filming, stunt parachutists Jake Lombard and B.J. Worth doubled for Bond and the pilot. (United Artists)

James "007" Bond (Jake Lombard) tracks after parachuting pilot (B.J. Worth) in free fall and captures life-saving Strato-Flyer rig, buckling it on just in the nick of time. (United Artists)

of his body position relative to the camera, and remain properly oriented geographically to the ground and the sun. Deluca served as the primary free fall photographer.

Though historically producers may have taken advantage of fliers, the studios are not out to kill pilots and pilots are not out to commit suicide. But according to Frank Pine, some stuntmen are just plain accident prone. They either kill themselves or go broke.

Pine's advice to anyone breaking into the business is to identify with an established organization specializing in motion pictures.

"You really need an organization behind you to survive," said Frank, "and you need personal integrity for safety."

A former Navy patrol plane commander and now one of the movie industry's most experienced aerial camera pilots, Pine went to work for Paul Mantz in 1959. Because of an extensive flight test background, Pine's first assignment was pilot of the Mantz-modified B-25 "borate bomber" used for fighting forest fires. However, Frank quickly transitioned into movie flying, soon piling up an impressive list of film credits for his work both before and behind the cameras. He knew his boss as well as anybody, perhaps better than most.

"I got along with Paul fine, I treated him like an admiral," said Pine, who retired from the Navy in 1955. "He wanted someone to back him up, not second-guess him. Too many pilots have a proclivity for asserting their ideas, telling other pilots how to fly. You didn't do that with Paul. Yet he had the respect of most everyone; the few who thought of him as a hotshot didn't count. He was a perfectionist—a hard taskmaster. And Paul always flew like a champion . . ."

Pine is still steeped in Navy. In fact, he equates a film production company's "pecking order" with the Navy's chain of command. He sees the producer as a flag officer representing the "money people." The director is in charge,

so he commands. Next, the production manager might be comparable to a ship's executive officer. However, in studio hierarchy the first assistant director, or "operations officer," will generally outrank the production manager.

"That's why we usually deal with the first assistant director; he's the man who gets things done," said Pine. "He controls the people, the equipment, the logistics—and he can hire and fire."

Some aviation firms and a few "independents" specializing in movie work advertise their services in the film industry's several marketing reference guides, such as the *Pacific Coast Studio Directory,* the *Studio Blu-Book* and *Kemps International Motion Picture and Television Yearbook.* But the vagaries of film schedules prevent all but a hand-

Close-up of Roger Moore as James Bond as he struggles with pilot of twin turboprop. In the film, Bond is subsequently shoved all the way out the door, sans parachute. (United Artists)

Rande Deluca, primary free fall photographer on *Moonraker*, joins up with Jake Lombard, right, and B.J. Worth. Note special 35mm movie camera with widescreen lens. (Peter Boettgenbach)

ful of established regulars from making a career of movie flying. The work is sporadic, and with few exceptions most of the pilots have fulltime jobs outside the motion picture industry. Yet flying for the films can be highly challenging and profitable, offering risk and reward in equal portions.

Pine stressed that film budgets are tight; even the shortest action sequence can be extremely costly. There is very little margin for error, particularly when an expensive set is to be destroyed in one blazing aerial bombardment. Usually there's only one "take," and when the action starts, everyone has to re-

spond with lightning reflexes. A single mistake could cost hundreds of thousands of dollars in wasted time and effort.

Making aviation movies is a dynamic business. Not only are lives at stake, but very often in period films irreplaceable vintage aircraft are involved. A director's zeal for creating a spectacular effect must always be tempered by the reality of what can or cannot be done safely.

And what does it take to be a good movie pilot?

The late Frank Tallman, who was regarded as tops in the field, never worked with daredevils because "most of them think with their egos rather than their heads." He wanted his fliers to be thoroughly professional—pilots who knew their own limitations as well as the limitations of the aircraft they flew. But the requirements of Frank Pine go even further.

"For the type of precision work most scripts call for today, I prefer mature ex-military pilots who have the experience with 'big-bore' aircraft few civilian-trained fliers can accumulate. They breed confidence in their fellow pilots by having that special ability to know what every plane will do in any attitude or airspeed. They've been around and know the difference between stunting and good flying."

Pine should know. He is equally skilled at flying on both sides of the camera. In *Catch-22* he flew as Tallman's B-25 wingman in the dangerous mass takeoff scenes. And more recently he ditched a Ryan Navion in the ocean for an episode in the Universal TV film *Family Flight.*

James S. "Jim" Appleby, Jim Gavin, Art Scholl and Ted Janczarek are four accomplished pilots who well fit Pine's definition of the ideal movie precision pilot. Jim Appleby, in fact, retired from the Air Force in 1963 and soon joined the Tallmantz organization, where he became general manager and chief pilot. He served as lead pilot and chief coordinator on *Catch-22,* which racked up 1,350 flying hours

Roger Moore lookalike Jake Lombard exits jump plane to begin an exciting air-to-air film sequence for *Moonraker*. Lombard also works as a helicopter ski guide. (Rande Deluca)

"Pilot" B.J. Worth in free fall wearing suit-parachute specially designed for *Moonraker* by Canadian chute-maker Zeke Zahar. Worth is also an accomplished filmmaker. (Peter Boettgenbach)

without scratching an airplane. (The only serious incident during the filming of *Catch-22* in Mexico occurred when cinematographer Johnny Jordan fell to his death from the tail turret of a B-25 camera plane being flown by Frank Pine. Jordan, who had previously lost a leg in a helicopter accident in Japan, seldom wore a parachute or even a safety harness while he worked.)

In 1972, Appleby and his attractive wife Zona, who also flies, formed their own company, Antique Aero, Ltd., which specializes in building to order full-scale replicas of World War I aircraft. Located on Flabob Airport in Riverside, California, Antique Aero's customers include museums and a cross-section of aviation interests in business, industry and the professions. Jim and Zona also perform in air shows, movies, and an occasional television commercial. (They've done Thunderbird spots for Ford, as one example.)

Movie fans, especially aficionados of the "flying flick," may well remember the thrilling final dogfight sequence in *The Great Waldo*

Pepper. That was Appleby flying the Sopwith Camel against Frank Tallman in the Fokker Triplane. (In the story Waldo is supposed to engage the German ace in mock combat for a 1930s era film company, but the contest turns into a death duel.) Appleby also did much of the flying in *The Stunt Man,* a Melvin Simon production, released in 1980. (In the fall of 1980 Jim Appleby suffered multiple fractures and other painful injuries in the crash of his Fokker Dr. 1 triplane during an air show in Las Vegas, Nevada. The accident occurred when the slipstream of a Nieuport 28 he was chasing in a mock dogfight flipped him near the ground, too low for a safe recovery. In the same show, stuntman Ralph Wiggins also sustained multiple breaks as a result of a "pulloff" style parachute jump from an altitude of about 300 feet.)

Art Scholl, a national and international aerobatic champion, is an ex-teacher who runs a successful flying school when not performing in air shows or doing movie work. He's as at home in gliders, warbirds and experimental aircraft as he is in his famous aerobatic Super Chipmunk, and has made several sensational appearances on ABC-TV's *That's Incredible*.

According to Scholl, many young pilots interested in flying for the movies know little of the personal discipline required to become a truly proficient flier. "They hear about the good money and glamour and think all it takes is the guts to do it," said Art. But the prospective movie pilot, Scholl cautions, must first understand the countless hours of training, the mental conditioning and the experience that is necessary to "make an airplane do exactly what you want it to do *every time.*"

Don Caltvedt, left, who also doubled for Roger Moore, and B.J. Worth show internal construction of suit-parachutes used in *Moonraker*. They feature low-profile designs. (Rande Deluca)

Jim Appleby, an experienced motion picture pilot, and his pretty wife Zona now build World War I aircraft on order at their Antique Aero shops in Riverside, Cal. (James S. Appleby)

Art also won plaudits for his flying in *Waldo Pepper.* In 1979 he shared honors with Ted Janczarek, a Continental Airlines captain, for their brillant sailplane and fixed-wing flying in *The Sky Trap,* a two-hour NBC television movie produced for *The Wonderful World of Disney* series. Ted himself is a relative newcomer to the ranks of Hollywood fliers, but his expertise with powered aircraft and gliders has already attracted the attention of every major studio in town. He has appeared in several feature films, and was one of the "regulars" in the *Black Sheep* series. In an interview with *Air Progress* magazine publisher Edwin Schnepf, the veteran airline pilot had this to say:

"Breaking into movie work isn't as hard as it may seem. I believe air show and competitive aerobatic experience is a great help because it helps hone the skills of performer and showman. You learn what pleases a crowd of judges and this attitude works well with movie directors. You have to cooperate with everyone on a movie set. You're part of a team of highly trained professionals. You have to know what they want and how to give it to them."

The Sky Trap featured some of the most spectacular and breathtaking glider flying ever filmed, largely to the credit of Jim Gavin, who not only directed the aerial sequences but piloted the camera platforms as well (a Bell Jet-Ranger helicopter and an ex-Air Force T-28). The picture cost over $1.6 million to make, with more than half the footage either in flight or around Rosamond Airport near Tucson, Arizona, the location for much of the shooting. Most of the aerial scenes, however, were taken over the northern expanse of the Mojave Desert, within the confines of California's Red Rock Canyon.

Sky Trap is an adventure story dealing with a financially troubled private airport, the sport of soaring, and a couple of U.S. Customs Service officers chasing some airborne drug smugglers. The aircraft involved in the film included the versatile Polish Wilga high wing monoplane, a Piper Lance, a Bellanca Citabria, two Blanik sailplanes, a Cessna 180 "tow tug" and the T-28. The JetRanger photo ship, a key to the excellent cinematography, did not appear on camera.

Gavin's association with the Walt Disney studios dates back to the early 1960s when he worked both helicopter and fixed-wing aircraft for *The Cat from Outer Space.* And as first assistant to *Sky Trap* producer-director-writer Jerome "Jerry" Courtland, Gavin headed the second unit location team of some 75 people, including pilots, technicians, "gaffers" and cameramen.

It's worth noting that the story outline was Jerry Courtland's answer to a long search for a plot perfectly suited to both Disney TV and his own hobby—flying. Jerry is an accomplished sailplane pilot in his own right, as is his son Chris, who flew some of the glider scenes. One of the other pilots recruited for *Sky Trap* was Tom Friedkin, whose father started Pacific Southwest Airlines (PSA). Flying the T-28 one day, Friedkin clipped a Joshua

tree on one of his low "passes," damaging the leading edge of his plane's outer left wing panel. Temporary field repairs were quickly made and, as they say in the trade, the show went on.

Gavin found the sailplanes to be a bit of a problem in production because they could make only one pass close to the ground on each flight. Moreover, the aerial shots were taken during some of the most difficult and trying weather conditions imaginable. The air was hot and cold, windy and calm, turbulent and smooth.

Despite the frustrations, Gavin's outstanding work on *Sky Trap* proved once again

One of Hollywood's busiest pilots, Art Scholl, pictured here with "Aileron," his mascot, also teaches aviation and operates a flying service. He is a former world aerobatic champion. (Edward H. Wood)

Filming Disney's *Sky Trap*, Tom Friedkin, left, clipped a "high flying" tree with his T-28 camera plane. Jim Gavin, center, and Art Scholl examine wing leading edge patch. (James W. Gavin)

why this native Californian is in such demand as a director, stunt coordinator, cameraman and pilot. In fact, today he is specializing in widely diversified action sequences, whether in the air or on the ground. Some of his rapidly growing list of motion picture and television credits (including the TV series *Emergency, The Rockford Files, Adam 12, McCloud, Barnaby Jones, The Six Million Dollar Man* and others) had little or nothing to do with aviation, except for the helicopters that might have been used to film car chases and other outdoor thrill scenes.

But all of Gavin's expanding activities in film production, particularly in the directorial fields, have evolved out of his experience in aviation, Jim told us recently.

A veteran of Korea where he flew Army "choppers" and fixed-wing L-5 and L-19 aircraft, Jim Gavin got into filming back in 1959 while flying for a helicopter outfit called MGA Air Services, based at Torrance, California. He happened to be piloting a new turbocharged Bell (model 47-G-3) helicopter at Lake Tahoe, under contract to the U.S. Forest Service, at the same time John Huston was shooting *The Misfits* there. Huston wanted some helicopter footage of wild horses near the old Stead Air

Force Base on the outskirts of Reno, Nevada. (Scripted by Arthur Miller, *The Misfits* starred Clark Gable, Marilyn Monroe and Montgomery Clift.)

"We were able to take the job as long as it didn't interfere with firefighting," said Gavin. "Incidentally, Paul Mantz was doing the flying with a Gypsy Moth on that film."

From there, Jim Gavin went on to become one of the most versatile action directors and camera plane pilots in Hollywood. Highly creative and imaginative, he knows cinematic requirements from both sides of the camera. His special talent for directing aerial action was perhaps best demonstrated by his work in the *Baa Baa Black Sheep* television series, which starred Robert Conrad as Gregory "Pappy" Boyington, the commander of VMF 214. Flying a specially-equipped North American T-28 with both flexible and wing-mounted cameras, Jim caught the exciting beat of aerial combat between Marine Corsairs and enemy Zeros in a manner that thrilled TV audiences for two seasons. (The show was retitled *Black Sheep Squadron* in its second year.)

In real life, Pappy Boyington left the

Frank Pine, Frank Tallman, and Tom Mooney in front of Vought F4U-4 Corsair used in filming *Black Sheep Squadron*. Tallman and Mooney were later killed in non-movie related crashes. (James W. Gavin)

Black Sheep Squadron, set in World War II, featured the Vought F4U Corsair. Due to the scarcity of flyable Corsairs, F4U-1, −4 (above), −5, −7, and FG-1 variants were all employed and mixed freely on the show. (U.S. Navy)

Marine Corps in 1941 to fight with Claire Chennault's American Volunteer Group (AVG), the famed "Flying Tigers." (The AVG flew rugged Curtiss P-40 Warhawks painted with menacing shark's teeth.) Later, the Tigers were disbanded and Boyington returned to the Marines where he was given his own squadron. Somewhat of a hellion in his own right, Pappy gathered together an odd assortment of incorrigibles and rejects from all the other squadrons, nicknaming them the "Black Sheep."

The pilots of VMF 214 were a motley crew indeed, but Pappy whipped them into a hard combat unit that soon blazed new trails of glory across Pacific skies. Boyington himself led by example, scoring 28 victories— including six planes shot down with the Flying Tigers in China. He was America's top Marine ace of the war.

Most of the aerial sequences for *Black*

Sheep were filmed above Southern California and offshore over the ocean, using a variety of warbirds. The Tallmantz B-25 was engaged for some of the shooting, but the vast majority of the footage was taken from a T-28 belonging to Tom Friedkin's Cinema Air. It was the same T-28 used later in the Disney movie *Sky Trap*.

The T-28's rear cockpit was stripped to provide working space for a cinematographer and his hand-held 35 (millimeter) Arriflex camera. Small remote TV scopes were installed in both cockpits so that Gavin and the cinematographer could monitor two fixed cameras slung in pods under the wings (including a remote-controlled zoom lens on one camera). For every film stunt they could expose three sets of film—two from the fixed cameras and one shot over Gavin's shoulder with the Arriflex. Because of the relatively small size of the average home TV screen, everything filmed had to be "bigger than life," as they say in Hollywood. The T-28 was also painted Navy blue to match the Corsairs, in case it ever "stuck its own thumb in front of the lens," so to speak.

There were some interesting problems on location at Indian Dunes, about 30 miles north of Los Angeles, where a narrow runway doubled as an island airstrip. It wasn't wide enough for more than one airplane. Thus, when the script called for a formation takeoff, one Corsair would start its roll down the strip, while another fighter—already airborne—would come alongside with its landing gear lowered. As a result of some careful cutting, the edited film would show what appeared to be several planes taking off at the same time.

Besides leasing his T-28 and some other aircraft to the *Black Sheep* producers, Friedkin also flew in the series. Among the show's "regulars" were two former Marine pilots who had actually flown with Boyington's fighter squadron (VMF 214) at the end of World War II—Glenn Riley and Tom Mooney.

Tragically, in the summer of 1978 Mooney was killed while flying a Grumman G-21A Goose for Antilles Air Boats, a Virgin Islands commuter air service founded by veteran airline pilot Charles F. Blair and his wife, the lovely actress Maureen O'Hara. Shortly afterward, on September 2, 1978, Blair himself

Jim Gavin, kneeling center, flanked by Frank Pine, left, and Tom Friedkin. Others in *Black Sheep* group include Glenn Riley, Tom Mooney, Ted Janczarek, Steve Hinton, Frank Tallman. Hinton holds world piston-powered aircraft speed record, set in the modified Red Baron "RB-51" Mustang. (James W. Gavin)

Cameraman J. Douglas Allen of Sound and Scene likes Arriflex 16 and 35mm models because either can be hand-held. Larger, heavier units, such as Mitchell, require special mounts. (Gates Learjet)

and three other persons were killed in the sudden crash of a sister ship. Despite her grief, Blair's widow undauntedly assumed the presidency of Antilles, the largest amphibian airline in the U.S., and kept its operations going.

Although the sophisticated lenses and cameras used today minimize much of the risk-taking, some film episodes can get a little hairy. In shooting *Black Sheep,* for instance, there was the constant problem of having the Japanese Zero fighters (actually North American T-6 trainers modified to look like Zeros) appear to fly faster than the F4U Corsairs.

"The pilots really had to know their stuff," said Gavin. "In steep banks, the Corsairs had to fly on the verge of a stall so the T-6s could keep up with them. Nor was it easy keeping

that T-28 slowed down as I tried to keep them both in my camera sights."

In many quarters Gavin is considered the best—and most expensive—of all the men who fly helicopters for motion pictures and television. It is said that he's often paid upwards of $3,000 for one day of special-effects filming and directing. But at first producers were afraid of choppers, believing them too dangerous. Also, film shot from "whirlybirds" was jerky. "We overcame those problems," Gavin said, "and now rotorcraft have become the hottest vehicle in TV."

Actually, the popularity of the helicopter as an aerial photo platform dates back to a system of camera mounts first developed in France. The French system pioneered the several sophisticated methods now available to isolate cameras from helicopter vibration. The present devices consist of either rubber shock mounts or springs and gimbels and a fulcrum suspended to the gimbel. And, contrary to a popular notion, there are no gyro mounts in current use. A fundamental requirement, of course, is the cinematographer's ability to manipulate the camera unit in any axis.

Cinematic equipment for commercial productions doesn't come cheap. A good camera system today, which would include either a single Mitchell or Arriflex 35mm camera (and the electronic accessories needed for operating and focusing the unit) will cost more than $100,000.

Gavin is convinced that it is sometimes easier and more economical to use a helicopter for filming a car chase, instead of setting up a series of ground-based cameras. He cites the example of "photographing a speeding car along the precipitous, winding highway south of Carmel, California, along the stark, sheer cliffs that lead into a foam-topped Pacific Ocean." The helicopter can cover the entire action with a single long "take" that might be cut into a number of flash clips on the screen. On the other hand, the time and logistics involved in supporting several camera locations would substantially increase shooting costs and location expenses.

But filming from helicopters is not without its risks, especially in aerial action scenes involving other aircraft.

Remember Johnny Jordan, the cameraman on *Catch 22* who fell out of a B-25 and was killed? Before his fatal accident, Jordan had lost a leg shooting a movie scene from a helicopter in Japan. He had a habit of letting his legs dangle outside the machine while he operated his camera. In this instance a second chopper that Jordan was photographing suddenly and inadvertently closed in, slicing off one of his lower limbs.

But perhaps the worst tragedy on a movie project in recent history happened over the Irish Sea in 1970, when a French Alouette collided with a reproduction of a German biplane fighter during the filming of an epic World War I dogfight for the Warner Brothers movie *Zeppelin*. Killed in the midair collision were England's famed aerial director, Skeets Kelly, whose credits included *The Blue Max* and *Around the World in 80 Days*; Gilbert Chomat, the noted French helicopter pilot and cameraman; Birch Williams, an assistant producer (and brother of film industry veteran Elmo Williams), and the Irish Air Force pilot flying the biplane.

Still, helicopters can be flown safely, as Gavin proves time and again; and their advantages in film work are many. Most people are accustomed to seeing police and emergency choppers land on roads and buildings—almost anywhere. Yet it's impossible to land a conventional aircraft on any kind of public street without reams of thoroughly documented special permission. Moreover, such approvals never come easy.

As this is written, Jim Gavin is preparing to handle the air activities for *High Road to China,* an adventure drama set in the early 1920s. The story is about a woman searching for her father, a munitions expert who is known to be in China. She hires an English ace to help find her dad and together they survive civil wars, roving bandits and other various perils. The script specifies use of several British Bristol F2B two-place tandem biplane fighters, affectionately known as the "Brisfit," one of the outstanding combat aircraft of World War I.

Six replicas of the Bristol were made for *High Road* by Vernon Ohmert of Ypsilanti, Michigan, a fulltime Learjet charter pilot who

Stuntman on right skid of Hughes 500C helicopter prepares to jump onto moving motor home as a police patrol Bell 47 tries to stop vehicle in *Spencer's Pilots*, a short-lived television series. (Art Scholl)

builds and flies planes for the movies on the side. Although one of the youngest in the new breed of motion picture fliers, Ohmert nevertheless has already compiled a portfolio of film credits, including *MacArthur, Cuba* and *Hanover Street*. He constructed the full-scale Bristol replicas for *High Road's* production company, Golden Harvest of Hong Kong, at a cost of approximately $750,000.

Two of the Bristols have already made their film debut, having been flown in *Death Hunt,* a movie filmed in the northern wilds of Canada. (It's a gripping tale based on the true story of how members of the Royal Canadian Mounted Police earned a reputation for always getting their man.) Equipped with pontoons instead of conventional landing gear, the planes received an acid test when they took off from a lake at an elevation of 6,400 feet, then climbed to 8,000 feet for air-to-air photography.

"The original Bristol F2B had a Rolls-Royce Falcon III engine that developed 275 horsepower," said Ohmert. "We used Ranger

154

200s and inverted them, but we also reduced the airframe weight by a substantial margin."

Ohmert started flying in 1967 as a junior in high school. Six years later he was in the aviation business to stay. For awhile he operated an air service at his hometown of Canon City, Colorado, where he piled up a lot of multiengine time in a Twin Beech and Lockheed Lodestar. Weekends and holidays found him hauling skydivers from all the sport parachute clubs in the surrounding area. Now he captains a sleek Learjet in charter service, carrying critically needed parts for the automotive industry out of Willow Run Airport at Detroit, Michigan. But between flights during much of 1979, Vern Ohmert built the Bristols.

In the summer of 1980, several of the planes were shipped by truck from a hangar at Ann Arbor, Michigan, to the Palomar Airport, California, near Jim Gavin's beach home. There the Bristols were to be modified, reassembled and flight tested at a cost of about $35,000 each.

One location that had been considered for some sequence in *High Road* is a dirt airstrip at Sleeping Indian Ranch, high on the western slope of the Rocky Mountains. Owned by Harry Combs, vice chairman of Gates Learjet Corporation and author of the book *Kill Devil Hill,* a definitive work on how the Wright brothers discovered flying, this beautiful spread would offer a magnificent setting for any motion picture requiring majestic, snow-capped mountain peaks as a backdrop. Interestingly, it is less than five miles from Ridgway, Colorado, a small community that served as the location for filming *True Grit,* Paramount's 1969 release starring the legendary John Wayne as the boozing, belching, old one-eyed frontier marshal "Rooster Cogburn." (While the late John Wayne will be remembered primarily for his long-running, two-fisted western roles, he also starred in a number of significant aviation films. Among his credits: *The Flying Tigers*, released in 1942; *Flying Leathernecks*, 1951; *Island in the Sky*, 1953; *The High and the Mighty*, 1954, and *Jet Pilot*, 1957. California's Orange County Airport was renamed John Wayne Airport in memory of the well-known actor, an area resident.)

The ranch strip at Sleeping Indian is 3,900 feet long (and one end is 225 feet lower than the other). Field elevation is 7,300 feet. Consequently, Jim Gavin, who is properly super-cautious with any machine that flies (or even moves), insisted on more thrust for the relatively low-powered Bristol biplane replicas. (Much of the $18-million *High Road*, starring Tom Selleck, was filmed in Yogoslavia in the spring of 1982.)

Years ago, airplane power-to-weight ratios were factors not always taken into account when planning aviation stunts. That's one reason why the men who fly for Hollywood's cameras today are a special breed of skilled airmen. They are the best in the business of bringing to theater and television screens the stark reality and excitement of flying. In unison with directors, cameramen, and special effects technicians, these men of action create thrilling aerial scenes that are often the most notable highlights of many TV and movie dramas.

True, they are carrying on in the tradition of the superb airmanship developed by pioneer movie fliers Ormer Locklear, Frank Clarke and Paul Mantz. But the new generation of pilots has added yet another dimension to their demanding profession—a practical, working knowledge of basic aeronautical principles. In the art and science of modern flight particularly as it is related to the making of motion pictures, an understanding of fundamental aerodynamics, propulsion systems and airframe construction is as vital to survival as the mental and physical application of piloting skill itself.

Even more important is the quality of judgment. The cemeteries are filled with pilots who either didn't have it or failed to use it well. In this sense, members of the Royal Canadian Air Force have an amusing but wise axiom that is especially apropos: "This aircraft is flown by a superior pilot. A superior pilot is one who stays out of trouble by using superior judgment to avoid situations that might damn well require the use of his superior skill."

Frank Pine, the wizard of Tallmantz Aviation and a veteran airman who thoroughly enjoys movie work, is as adamant on the subject of flying safety as anyone you'll ever meet. "Sure, we're all venturesome, and our business can be risky," observes Pine philosophically. "But I must say, this is not the *last* thing I'm going to do in my life."

Chapter 9

Bold Men and Big Iron

Jim Gavin had charge of all the aerial sequences for *Airport 79*, in which the "Joe Patroni" character (the gruff, tough, cigar-chewing mechanic played by George Kennedy) finds himself piloting the supersonic Concorde on a transatlantic crossing and beset by people who don't want the airplane to make it. It does, of course, but only after providing theatergoers with two hours of excitement.

Gavin estimates that location costs in Europe, including use of the airliner, Clay Lacy's Learjet photo plane—which was flown to Paris—and rented Bell JetRanger, came to more than $50,000 per flying hour. Jean T. Franchie, chief pilot for Aerospatiale (builders of the British/French SST) flew the Concorde during the filming. Gavin was so busy directing or flying the helicopter he didn't have a chance to copilot the faster-than-sound transport. But his longtime associate Larry Powell did. Powell, an ex-military flier who also works on Clint Eastwood productions, served as an aviation coordinator for the *Airport* movies.

According to Gavin, the assignment involving Concorde was the most difficult he has ever handled, principally because of the very high cost of aircraft and staff on location. "There's no room for error under those conditions," he said. But he added that the footage obtained abroad was "absolutely spectacular."

The JetRanger was used as a stationary camera platform over the Alps as the Concorde made its runs. At about 250 knots the transport is like a big jet fighter, enabling Gavin and his crew to show a good relative speed from the helicopter. For other shots they used Clay Lacy's Learjet equipped with "Astrovision," a unique, remote-controlled camera system capable of filming high performance aircraft in any direction.

Gavin had similar responsibilities on *Airport 77*. As second unit director for *Airport 75* he supervised all the complex flying scenes of the Boeing 747 which, in the story, collides almost head-on with a twin-engine Beechcraft Baron. The horrifying accident incapacitates the airliner's flight crew. Another pilot (the indestructable Charlton Heston) is rushed to a rendezvous with the 747, then is transferred from a helicopter to the transport's damaged flight deck where he takes over the controls and saves all on board.

In reality, stuntman Joe Canuck was lowered to within 18 feet of the 747's nose, although on film it appears he completes the transfer. The footage of this thrilling scene was shot near Salt Lake City, Utah. Gavin managed to fly the 747 while on location, re-

Jim Gavin in cockpit of T-28 camera plane. Much of his work for Hollywood is done with helicopters, such as *Sky Heist*, a movie featuring Los Angeles sheriff's men chasing thieves.

porting that at light weight it had a stall speed of 95 knots and flew well for the air-to-air sequences at 120 knots. He said the hardest part was taxiing the huge aircraft with no outside references from where he sat in the cockpit so high above the ground.

Incidentally, the "real" Joe Patroni, the man on whom the *Airport* movie character was based, is Roy Davis, head of maintenance at TWA's facilities in Chicago. Although not as large physically as George Kennedy, his make-believe counterpart in the series, Davis also chews a cigar and he actually did what Patroni does in the first *Airport* film—get a stuck airliner out of the snow. Not only that, Roy was the one who convinced Kennedy he should learn to fly. George took the advice,

soon had his pilot's license and he now flies his own Beechcraft Bonanza in the frequent business travel necessary to his career and for personal transportation. (Universal's *Airport* theme may have run its course. A 1980 Paramount release titled *Airplane*, which cost some $3 million to make, spoofs the series. A light, fast and hilariously funny comedy, it was written for the screen and directed by Jim Abrahams and David and Jerry Zucker.)

Like others in the field, Jim Gavin has his own ideas about what makes a good aviation film. He sees a potential market for a new war movie structured around a strong, well-developed central character in the concept of the original *Wings* or Henry King's *Twelve O'Clock High*, a fine World War II film on bombers. In the latter, for example, a stubborn flying general is given the assignment of rebuilding a bomber group whose shattered morale under heavy losses threatens to discredit daylight bombing and undermine the whole aerial offensive against a German-occupied Europe.

Based on the novel by Sy Bartlett and Bernie Lay, Jr., the 20th Century-Fox release (1949) stars Gregory Peck as the general who goes about his job with such fierce passion that every pilot accepts an invitation to apply for transfer. But this shock treatment finally pays off in bombing results, a grudging admiration for the officer and the long hoped-for *esprit de corps* in the bomber group. A *Time* magazine review of the period had this to say about *Twelve O'Clock High*:

"It successfully blends an artistry all too seldom shown by the Hollywood high commands . . . film has the uncommon merit of restraint. It avoids such cinemilitary booby traps as self-conscious heroics, overwrought battle scenes and the women left behind and picked up along the way. The general's fight to mend the morale of the group is a self-contained story so absorbingly pictured that some cinemagoers may feel a letdown when there seems nothing left to fight but Germans."

Gavin thinks Martin Caidin's novel *Whip*, the story of an intense Air Force captain

Author-pilot Martin Caidin in right seat of lead B-17 "somewhere over the ocean." His penchant for German war relics culminated in purchase and restoration of rare 1930s vintage Junkers Ju-52/3m. (Bill Mason)

(loosely based on the real-life "Pappy" Gunn) whose B-25 outfit fought with deadly effectiveness at treetop and wavetop level, ultimately becoming the proudest American unit in the Pacific, just might be adaptable to a screenplay. "I'd like to work on that one," said Gavin, his eyes gleaming. In fact, *Whip* has all the action, pace and accuracy of Caidin's companion volume, *The Last Dogfight*, which has already been acquired for a major motion picture.

Martin Caidin is no stranger to Hollywood, nor to flying. The prolific author of some 120 books, he is a commercial pilot, global adventurer, and a recognized authority on aeronautics and astronautics. He has been on the scene and behind the scenes of every manned flight into space, serving in various capacities as a reporter, broadcaster and even as a consultant to the U.S. government. Among Caidin's many novels, his *Marooned* was made into a movie, also starring Gregory Peck, and *Cyborg* was developed into the popular television series *The Six Million Dollar Man*.

Marooned, Caidin's first novel, was published by E.P. Dutton & Co. in 1964. An immediate success, it took six more years before the book could be done as a movie. But more important, it helped persuade Russia to take part in a joint Soviet-American space mission, which became the historic Apollo-Soyuz Test Project (ASTP) of 1975. Here's what happened:

In the spring of 1970 the new film *Marooned*, which shows how U.S. astronauts stranded in orbit are saved by a Russian spaceship, was previewed at a benefit in Washington, D.C. Among those in the audience was Philip Handler, then president of the National Academy of Sciences. Handler was so impressed by the movie that on a subsequent trip to Moscow he glowingly described it to his counterparts in the Soviet Academy of Sciences.

"That an American film should portray a Soviet cosmonaut as the hero who saves American lives came to the Russians as a distinct shock," Handler recalled.

Handler went on to make a strong plea for cooperation in space. Using the film to open his presentation, he explained how much easier rescues would be if the two space powers developed a common docking mechanism. In *Marooned*, the cosmonaut had to leave his capsule and take a risky "space walk" before he could deliver oxygen to the Americans. The point was not lost on the Russians, who at that time were having trouble with their Soyuz spacecraft. They promised to recommend the idea to their political leaders.

Time magazine reported that less than two months later the Soviets told Handler they were willing not only to expand scientific contacts but to begin discussing the design of a common docking mechanism as well. Shortly thereafter, the two countries initiated formal negotiations for a joint space mission. Commented Caidin: "It's nice to know that a writer can sometimes influence the course of history."

In 1961 Caidin himself relived history. Sixteen years after the last shot was fired in World War II, he and a few dedicated, determined associates procured three aging B-17 bombers and flew them to England for the filming of *The War Lover*, a Columbia Pictures release based on John Hersey's best selling novel.

"The whole idea of flying three decrepit Flying Fortresses across the Atlantic was utterly mad," Martin told us. "Not flying three such airplanes, for the B-17 is a grand old girl indeed. But the ones we selected were ground-loving, scabrous dump heaps that had lain in Texas and Arizona soil for so many years they'd sunk into the asphalt and desert sand where they had been left to rot."

Heading out to recreate World War II offensive against enemy plants for *The War Lover*, this B-17 and thousands like it were the mainstay of America's bomber forces. Unlike most B-17s, however, this one survived not only fighters and flak but the most destructive enemy of all—the scrapper's torch. (Caidin Archives)

Because Hollywood is the center of the film industry, its nearby airports house many of the specialized airplanes needed for films. With the exception of the Confederate Air Force (a "ghost squadron" of flyable World War II combat aircraft maintained at their "Rebel Field" headquarters in Harlingen, Texas), movie-makers can find just about any vintage type they want from nearby Orange County, Van Nuys, Palomar, Santa Paula, Chino or Riverside.

But the best sources for "big iron" (war surplus multiengine bombers and transports) back in those days—and even today—were the aircraft "boneyards" of the American Southwest. That's where Caidin and an enterprising Australian named Gregory R. "Greg" Board found the 17s.

Columbia Pictures publicized one of the four-engine planes, a B-17G model, as the same aircraft used by General Douglas MacArthur as his personal transport. "It made a nice story," said Caidin, "but it was so much crap—like the derelict airplane." The two other "Forts" technically hadn't been B-17s at all.

Instead, they were Boeing PB-1W models designed for Naval search and rescue and adorned with monstrous plastic radomes that once housed radar antenna. By the time the airplanes arrived on location, the delivery expedition had become an epic that surpassed in excitement and events almost anything that would ever happen in the film!

"Greg Board, John Crewdson and Tim Clutterbuck were the instigators of all this madness," Caidin reflected. "And to think that Board led the whole affair across the ocean and most of the continent, and had never flown a B-17 in his life. But he could fly anything with wings on it. Anyone who could fly a Buffalo with the Royal Australian Air Force out of Rangoon and Singapore against the Zero fighter and live to tell about it is a brilliant flier and an incredibly lucky dude, to boot."

The people who restore or refurbish old airplanes agree there's only one right way to do it—and that is to do it *right*. Caidin admits he and his friends did it wrong. But he is quick to explain why:

"It's simple. Movie contracts for aircraft

are usually based on certain fixed fees involving the basic price of the planes and the cost of any work required to make them airworthy, plus the ferry crews and their expenses. So the less you spend on rebuilding the ironmongers, the more you make when they arrive at their contractual destination. The net result is doing the least for the most, which is another way of saying you're begging for disaster."

There were frequent—and scary—mechanical problems. Propellers suddenly flew off. Douglas DC-3 (the mid-1930s vintage airliner) parts and equipment were liberally mixed with Boeing B-17 components. In fact, any spare part that even *looked* like it had a chance of making it went on the machine.

Caidin recalled the time the entire plexiglass nose of John Crewdson's bomber suddenly collapsed in flight, instantly transforming the Fort into a "shrieking, clanging, rumbling, shaking wind tunnel." Since most of the other parts and systems were also marginal, Crewdson did a marvelous job of bringing the old warbird in safely. Greg Board, incidentally, flew his first flight in a B-17 solo. "He sucked on a bottle of fine whiskey in a motel room, read the manual, went out early the next morning and took off alone," said Martin. "And on

Three aging B-17s were restored for *The War Lover* at Ryan Field near Tucson. Aero American owner Gregory Board contracted the job, which involved ferrying the bombers to England. (Caidin Archives)

Greg Board, second from left, wonders if Flying Fortress he's bought will ever get off the ground. Other pilots and mechanics ponder problems of rejuvenating the old bomber. (Caidin Archives)

takeoff he lost an engine. He punched the prop into feather and continued right on flying, as nonplussed as one might imagine."

The exciting account of how the three old bombers were ferried to England is vividly told in Martin Caidin's nonfiction book *Everything But the Flak*, published in 1964 by Duell, Sloan & Pearce. But not "everything" went into the story, Martin stated recently. For example, getting across the Atlantic alive became such a concern that five "crewmen"—publicity people, photographers and "Madison Avenue colonels"—withdrew in Newfoundland and returned to New York.

Two of the bombers didn't have adequate instrumentation so they flew wing on the 17 flown by Board and Caidin. Somewhere over the ocean the flight got caught in a nasty storm and had to descend to lower altitudes. The planes couldn't fly through the storm because two of them lacked the proper navigation equipment for instrument flight; they relied solely on visual contact. Said Caidin:

"There we were, three B-17s flying formation out in the middle of the Atlantic many years after World War II was over, right down on the deck, just pounding along—and I mean we were right *on* the waves—so close we were sucking water into the airplanes with the props. We came around a cloud bank, the fog hanging right on the sea, and all of a sudden I was yelling 'Pull up! Pull up!' I grabbed the yoke and hauled like hell. There was a submarine conning tower right in front of us. We missed it by about two feet . . ."

Caidin also stated that he will never forget seeing a face in the conning tower looking up, a white face with two big eyes and an open mouth. "What the poor S.O.B. told those people down in the sub, I'll never know," Martin added. "Never found out whose sub it was, although somebody in NATO sure raised hell over it. That was quite a trip."

Although *The War Lover's* headiest adventures may not have occurred in front of the cameras, the film offers some superb B-17 footage. Further, as in some other retrospective movies, doubts about the glory of war become abundantly clear. For among all the films that pronounce this fact of life, *The War*

Lover is one of the best. It stars Steve McQueen and Robert Wagner, with McQueen playing the superman pilot "Rickson" who has gone psycho for his B-17. Here's a sampling:

Wagner meets a British woman in a pub. She has lost her lover to combat and wears a patina of weariness with war that contrasted Britons with the eager Americans. McQueen horns in and attempts to monopolize the conversation.

She: "You're enjoying the war?"

He: "I enjoy my work."

She: "What is your work?"

He: "Lady, I belong to the most destructive group of men the world has ever known. That's my work."

B-17's plexiglass nose blew wide open in flight, turning the old bomber into a howling wind tunnel. Pilot John Crewdson carefully assesses damage—and counts his blessings. (Caidin Archives)

John Crewdson and Les Hillman prepare for Atlantic crossing in this stirring scene at Logan International Airport, Boston. Their destination: England and *The War Lover*. (Caidin Archives)

The girl (Shirley Ann Field) is unimpressed, and eventually falls in love with the quieter, more sensitive Wagner. But it turns out that McQueen is so bent on destruction he even tries to ruin Wagner's love affair. The movie quite deliberately portrays Rickson's (McQueen) psychosis as that of the hero gone berserk. At one point Wagner says, "Rickson represents the fine line that separates the hero from the psychopath."

For the actual filming, John Crewdson and a picked team of pilots and crewmen turned back the clock and duplicated the scenes of wartime bombing raids and air battles. Once on location, the old B-17s, identified for movie operations as "Blue One," "Blue Two" and "Blue Three," were restored to excellent flying condition. Ironically, it then became John

Crewdson's task to smash some parts of the bombers so as to recreate the damage they had received from the effects of enemy flak and fighters. Much of this fell to Les Hillman, a miracle worker when it came to fixing or wrecking fine aircraft.

"On several occasions Hillman and his ground crews so mangled the bombers for flight scenes that John refused to allow anyone to enter the airplane with him and, like Greg, he took repeatedly to the air as the sole occupant of the four-engine bomber," wrote Caidin in *Everything But the Flak*. "He made three-engine takeoffs to simulate—with full and literal realism—engine failures in the story taking shape before the cameras. He did extensive low-level work over the English Channel with two engines dead, and it might be said that our long flight to England prepared him admirably for these sequences."

Crewdson flew the Fortresses with engines dead and propellers feathered. When John landed, Les Hillman and his gang battered an engine and prop into crushed, useless junk. Then Crewdson would take off again to fly more scenes. He flew the Forts with bomb doors smashed, landing gears jammed, wheels dangling unevenly and wings slashed—all to show "battle damage" as inflicted by enemy gunfire.

No one was killed or injured flying the bombers that had been brought back to life. With tragic irony, however, the noted British sport parachutist, Mike Reilly, died jumping from Crewdson's B-17. Reilly, doubling as a crew member, was simulating an emergency bailout over the English Channel. He landed in the water safely, but weighted down with heavy gear, he drowned before rescuers could reach him.

Shortly after *War Lover* shooting ended, Blue Two and Blue Three were scrapped and their best parts and pieces put into Blue One,

the same B-17 that Greg Board and Caidin had flown over to England. The rebuilt airplane was now destined for Hollywood and another movie. Caidin rejoined the crew in Boston, and from there they headed out across the United States once again. What they believed would be an easy flight soon became the hairiest of all their Flying Fortress adventures.

"We were over Texas, rumbling along nicely, when the sky ahead turned into a lemon pie—the *inside* of one, that is," said Caidin. "We went from 8,000 feet to 12,000 to 14,000; we were smack in the damnedest sandstorm you ever saw, it was absolutely opaque."

Martin remembers that radio reports told of zero-zero visibility on the ground, so they couldn't go down. Nor could they go left or right. The only way to go was over the stuff, he said, "because if you flew inside it, the sand would tear hell out of the engines and you'd overheat and fire would loom and all that sort of thing. Someone suggested we might think about bailing out, but that would be stupid because we didn't have any chutes and we were all of the opinion that the only thing that falls out of the sky is birdcrap and idiots . . ."

Crewdson kept the bomber climbing to 20,000 feet, then to 22,000. He dragged it on up to 24,000 feet, only to discover they didn't have enough oxygen aboard. Everyone in the airplane was moving slowly, loosening his clothing and watching the man in the pilot's seat, anticipating that hypoxia might very well nail them all. Also, riding above the sandstorm, they nearly froze to death. Two crewmen had already passed out; the rest were breathing deep and slow, frequently relieving one another at the controls.

"Finally we were over the edge of it, and you could see the stuff billowing ahead like a great wave of sandy foam," Martin related. "We started down, and by the time we were back at 16,000 feet our lungs were filling up again. I swear, flying those B-17s for the movies was dull compared with just getting them there."

Two years after the B-17 escapade Greg Board called Caidin and told him the old gang, John Crewdson, Tim Clutterbuck and the rest, plus a newcomer, John "Jeff" Hawke, were shooting a movie in England called *633 Squadron* and would be tooling around in British de Havilland Mosquito bombers. Greg said they needed a B-25 for some paratrooper scenes—or rather, dropping saboteurs into Norway—and asked if he, Caidin, would like to help fly it over. Martin pondered the question for all of half a second and shouted, "You bet your sweet ass!"

Caidin and Board met at Logan in Boston and together they looked over the twin-engine North American B-25J Mitchell parked on the ramp. Martin crawled up inside the fuselage and found what he dreaded most—a cockpit cluttered not only with switches, dials and gauges, but with rust, dust and illegible markings everywhere. Noting Martin's anxiety, Greg muttered something about the ship being in "good shape," although the right inboard tank leaked a lot when it was full. The trick was to fill the tanks to the very brim, Board added, then fire up and take off like a scalded cat so no fuel would be wasted.

The flight plan called for flying Boston to the RCAF field at Goose Bay, Newfoundland, then leaping off and overflying Greenland, straight into Iceland where they would land and remain overnight. Out of Goose Bay they cruised at 14,000 feet, with a 50-knot wind pushing their tail. But coming across the southern tip of Greenland on a beautiful July afternoon the world suddenly went white. "We were in the middle of a howling blizzard," Caidin recalled. "It got our attention, especially when we felt rumbles and shakes as the engines began icing up."

Board: "We'd better use some carburetor heat."

Caidin: "Right."

Board: "Okay, apply carb heat."

Caidin: "Sure. Just tell me where the controls are."

Board: "I don't know. I thought you knew."

Caidin: "I don't know. I thought *you* knew."

The engines continue rumbling and shaking. Now they start coughing and popping . . .

Caidin: "Where's the flight manual?"

Board, jerking a thumb behind him: "Somewhere back there with the emergency gear. I think I know where it is. You fly and I'll look."

Caidin, to himself: "Interesting. From the right seat the artificial horizon requires a special technique. You've got to hold the airplane—according to the indicator—in a 15-degree right bank to be sure the airplane is level. Oh, brother, that's wonderful! Where the hell is Board? Those damn engines . . ."

Board, returning to his seat and flourishing the flight manual: "Here it is. Hang in there."

Board opens the manual and the yellow paper crumbles. Caidin invokes the name of the Savior.

Board: "Amen." (*He throws away the glop in his hands.*)

The two pilots pulled and pushed and poked and turned everything until they found the carburetor heat, and the whole time they were flying blind. But the heat came on and it stayed on until they were out of the snow. They landed in Iceland, refueled, slept a few hours and took off. Caidin flew the final leg from the right seat (using the "cock-eyed artificial horizon" as primary attitude reference) while Board catnapped and talked idly with other airmen who weren't in solid cloud.

Messerschmitt Bf. 108b owned and flown by Martin Caidin doubled for Germany's renowned single-seat Bf. 109E fighter in *633 Squadron*, a 1964 United Artists release. (Bill Mason)

Finally they arrived at their destination, Bovington, landing between rain showers.

United Artists released *633 Squadron* in 1964. The movie stars Cliff Robertson and features some incredible footage of the Mosquitos and a bunch of Messerschmitt Bf. 108b *Taifuns* (playing the role of Bf. 109s, Germany's great fighter of World War II). The story revolves around a strike against a Nazi plant in Norway, but outstanding flying sequences make the picture.

Caidin got checked out in a 108b, flew in some of the attack scenes ("beating up the field and strafing planes and people and hangars") and ended up buying the two-place Messerschmitt, complete with Luftwaffe military markings. The same plane also appeared in *The Longest Day*; those who saw the movie may remember the scene in which a German

fighter roars along the invasion beachhead, gunning Allied troops. That was Martin's 108. Former Royal Air Force pilot John Hawke, accompanied by his pretty fiancée, Jean Cullum, flew the single-engine plane back to the United States, via Iceland, Greenland and Canada. (A second 108 flying with Hawke was forced down on the coast of Labrador. Its crew, pilot Francis Freeman and British photographer Robin Carruthers, were rescued the next day.)

Another plane used in filming *The Longest Day* was a British Supermarine Spitfire Mark IX that saw action in World War II. It is now the mainstay of actor Cliff Robertson's fleet of vintage aircraft, which includes a Messerschmitt Bf.108b, three Tiger Moths and a French Stampe. He also owns a twin-engine Beechcraft Baron.

168

Although Robertson became enamored with aviation as a boy, his acting career intervened. (He won an Academy Award in 1968 for his portrayal of the title role in *Charly*, but is perhaps better remembered as a young John F. Kennedy in *PT-109*.) He returned to flying while working on *633 Squadron* in England and France. "I bought a Tiger Moth—it's easy to fall in love with old biplanes; they have personality." Later he acquired the Spitfire from the Belgian Air Force when he heard it might be cannibalized. "It's not only a fine airplane, it virtually saved Western civilization," said Cliff. "The RAF could not have won the Battle of Britain without the Spitfire."

Most of Robertson's recent experience in aviation film has been confined to flying old or new airplanes in movies he has directed, written and acted in himself. He flew a Tiger Moth in *J. W. Coop* and *The Fortune*. More recently he piloted his Stampe in a television special celebrating the history of flight. Robertson also narrated the hour-long show, titled *A Place of Dreams*. The program originated in the Smithsonian Institution's National Air and Space Museum and premiered over the Public Broadcasting Service (PBS) network in December 1979.

Robertson's latest film, *The Pilot*, is based on the novel by Robert P. Davis (William Morrow & Company, 1976). It is a convincing but terrifying story of a highly skilled commer-

Caidin later bought and restored an extremely rare Junkers Ju. 52/3m, seen here during lull in filming "wartime attack" by German paratroops for television production. Caidin is in flight suit. (Paul Robert Brown)

T-28, P-38, and T-6 make "firing runs" at Martin Caidin's Ju. 52 during television filming in Florida. Caidin found the historic, rust-covered plane on a jungle airstrip in Ecuador, and his book *The Saga of Iron Annie* details the fascinating story of its recovery and restoration. (Caidin Archives)

cial airline pilot whose dependence on alcohol threatens the lives of his passengers and crew. Cliff not only acted in the movie, he directed it as well.

Cliff Robertson, Jim Gavin and Martin Caidin are among the industry's leading critics of modern aviation filmmaking. Few movies today, in their opinion, show flying as it *really* is. The celluloid airplane means formula. If it is a war movie, certain predictable characters will die; if it's about civil aviation, pilots may die, but passengers usually survive—the airliner itself will be durable enough to fly through a building or sink in the sea without spilling a cocktail.

That's one reason Caidin decided to form his own production company, Ishtar Studios, named for the Babylonian goddess of love and war. (It's also the name of a continental feature on the planet Venus—Ishtar Terra.) By basing operations in his home state of Florida, he

figures he can turn out a winning war epic for about a third of what it would cost to produce the same film in Hollywood. His *Coke Machine*, an action adventure story of drug running with airplanes, boats and cars, might very well be Ishtar's first movie.

"The single most important element of a good motion picture is a great story," Caidin says. "Frank Capra taught me something. He said, 'Never use money as a crutch to make a movie, you'll end up with a sloppy film.' In other words, the story is the thing."

Caidin gives high marks to the 1952 London Film release called *Breaking the Sound Barrier*, a thinly disguised story of the late Geoffrey de Havilland's pursuit of the mysteries that lie beyond Mach 1. (*Test pilot:* "What happens to an airplane at the speed of sound?" *Engineer:* "I don't know, and I want to tell you something, Tony, no one in the world knows, either.") Ralph Richardson and Ann

Cliff Robertson—actor, pilot, and owner of a fine collection of antique aircraft, ranging from Tiger Moths to a World War II Spitfire. He flies several of them regularly.

London Film Productions' prophetic air drama of 1952, *Breaking the Sound Barrier*, forecast the day of supersonic air travel. It featured Ralph Richardson and Ann Todd, at right.

Todd star in the David Lear Production. Aerial units were directed by the talented Anthony Squire.

Anyone with a fondness for airplanes would enjoy *Sound Barrier*, which still appears now and then on PBS television or "The Late Late Show." Even the dialogue is believable. Says the British instructor to his student about to solo: "Try to get it down in one piece like a good chap." Asked how it went after diving a new jet, the apprehensive test pilot, hiding his

concerns, calmly replies, "A piece of cake."

The film makes the point that "exploring the unknown is always a little chancy." As is so often the case in real life when men are pitted against machine, the aircraft designer suffers personal hardship and tragedy in his quest to produce a supersonic plane. The horror of a doomed pilot in the final, fatal dive has rarely been depicted on film with the pungent and memorable quality of one scene showing the engineer playing back a tape of the last radio transmission while the pilot's widow races out, trying to cover her ears. It is a gripping portrayal of primal fear. (As good as *Breaking the Sound Barrier* is, it contains two gross inaccuracies: that the sound barrier was first broken in Britain, and that the proper thing to do when going transonic is to reverse the controls.)

Appropriately enough, the experimental plane in *Breaking the Sound Barrier* is named "Prometheus," the titan in Greek legend who stole fire from heaven as a gift for man. And though the movie was made nearly 30 years ago, it correctly foretold the day of 2,000 mph air travel.

Chapter 10
Aviation Film in Perspective

Over the years, motion pictures have done much to help publicize and popularize aviation. But in so doing, they have often distorted it. The common belief that most aircraft accidents are caused by equipment failure or bad weather stems partly from old movies in which heroic pilots safely land crippled or weather-battered planes.

Be it good or evil, the airplane is, in Hollywood, a device imposing its own imperatives upon characters and story. Put an airplane on the silver screen and it dominates the scene. The movie easily becomes "an airplane story," the symbol of defiance, destruction or disaster. In the minds of viewers, at least, it is almost as if the flying machine itself had turned into a wild animal or an active volcano.

In Warner Brothers' *Air Mail* of the early 1930s, a mail pilot is pictured trapped in a burning plane. His comrade shoots him to end his suffering. (This twist was adapted for *Waldo Pepper*, as well.) And in the original Paramount flick, *The Air Mail,* made in 1925, display advertising of the day boldly stated, "Not Snow, Nor Rain, Nor Wind, Nor Night, Can Stay the Pilot in His Flight." (Silent filmmaker Irvin Willat produced *The Air Mail* of 1925, which starred his wife, the exceptionally beautiful Billie Dove; Warner Baxter,

Mary Brian and Douglas Fairbanks, Jr. It has been reported that in 1930 Howard Hughes gave Willat more than $300,000 to divorce Billie Dove. Though "Howard and Billie" then became a Hollywood twosome, they never married. J.B. Alexander, aviation chief for *Hell's Angels*, taught Miss Dove to fly at Howard's request. Hughes, whom Billie termed "a brilliant air pilot and a first class golfer," also starred her in one of his own air epics, the 1932 Caddo-United Artists release, *Cock of the Air,* with Chester Morris and Charles Lederer. Willat survived Hughes—the rival who stole his wife—by precisely two weeks, both dying in 1976.)

As mentioned earlier, war offers the perfect setting for the celluloid airplane. It creates an endless state of emergency. On top of that, the allies are always the underdogs, vastly outnumbered by a better equipped, obscene enemy that regularly perpetrates atrocities on women and children. In fact, from the tremendous outpouring of aviation film with a war theme during the 1920s and '30s, one might think World War I was fought for the benefit of Hollywood.

Screenwriters also helped shape the early image of airplane pilots as fearless supermen who spend most of their non-flying hours swigging booze and chasing women. In *The Legion of the Condemned*, Bill Wellman's 1928 sequel to *Wings*, the hokey bravado is laid on with a steam shovel. (John Monk Saunders wrote the original story.)

Gary Cooper stars in *Legion* as the "sky raider" in love with a flapper spy, Fay Wray. It's the tale of a "flying escadrille" of young men who have incurred the wrath of blondes and police, a sort of aerial Foreign Legion of youths who want to die in order to forget. Returning from their flying sorties, the lads retire to their favorite drinking resort, build tiny coffins on their tables, put candles at all four corners and have general orgies of self-pity. Even in 1928, *Liberty* movie reviewer Frederick James Smith questioned whether "daredevil aviators acted like this."

But for aviation buffs, especially, the fly-ing action is always good film fare. Another outstanding air movie of bygone years was MGM's 1935 release, *West Point of the Air,* also written by John Monk Saunders. It starred Wallace Beery as the pioneer Army flier whose son, Robert Young, grows up in the military tradition.

Produced with the cooperation of the U.S. government, the film's skies were filled with scores of Army airplanes. Such spectacular flying and parachute jumping scenes, in fact, made *West Point of the Air* a model of its type. Yet as a sign of the times back in the mid-thirties, one reviewer commented that the "picture is another in the entertaining war propaganda series in which the War Department cheerfully cooperates, services freely given." (Martin Caidin take note: While making this film in 1935, Metro-Goldwyn-Mayer

MGM's flying flick *Pursuit*, directed by Edwin L. Marin, featured Chester Morris, Sally Eilers and Scotty Beckett. A weak story line was helped by the exciting air action. (Metro-Goldwyn-Mayer)

seriously considered moving its studios to Florida because of high California taxes.)

During World War II, a number of air action films were made with the approval and cooperation of the War Department, Warner Brothers' *Air Force* (1943) and *God Is My Copilot* (1945) as notable examples.

Air Force is the saga of a B-17 named *Mary Ann* and the men who gave her a soul. In the story, the aerial battlewagon had a blind date with destiny, flying smack into the war's first explosions in the Pacific. *God Is My Copilot* is the autobiography of Robert L. Scott, an Air Force fighter pilot (13 kills) who flew in China with Claire Chennault and his Flying Tigers. Scott's own shark-nosed P-40 and two dozen B-25s were used in making the picture. He also served as a technical advisor.

Above and Beyond, starring Robert Taylor (who was also a pilot) as Col. Paul Tibbets, is saturated with footage of B-17s, B-26s, B-29s, C-47s and C-54s—a terrific collection for one film. Tibbets piloted the *Enola Gay*, the B-29 that dropped the first atomic bomb on Hiroshima. In 1980 Tibbets would be portrayed for film once again, this time by Patrick Duffy ("Bobby Ewing" of TV's *Dallas*) in the NBC-TV movie titled, appropriately enough, *Enola Gay*. For the film, the Confederate Air Force provided two B-29s and the Air Force allowed the use of Davis-Monthan AFB.

United Artists' 1969 release *The Thousand-Plane Raid* is technically good. (The bombing run sequences include stock footage—actual combat film mixed with newsreel clips.) The story deals with the first of the massive air strikes over principal German targets in 1943. While it had all the potential for an exciting movie, it turned into little more than a stereotype adventure that lacks an in-

Wallace Beery, a pilot in real life, with Roscoe Turner. Beery and Clark Gable starred in MGM's epic *Helldivers*, for which the U.S. Navy's Fighting One did most of the flying. (Beech Aircraft)

For *Gallant Journey*, a 1946 release based on pioneer J.J. Montgomery's life, producer William Wellman used old photos for reference, like this 1905 shot of "JJ," left, and his glider.

volvement with any of characters. Christopher George plays the harsh, hard-nosed commander of a bombardment group who masterminds an often-rejected but finally-realized plan to send a wave of 1,000 B-17s to destroy in one giant assault Germany's main aircraft manufacturing center.

In *The Bridges at Toko-Ri*, a first-rate military drama of the Korean War (1954), not even the protagonist escapes an awful fate: the late William Holden's Grumman F9F gives out just one ridgeline short of the open sea and certain rescue. In contrast, an earlier film about another war, titled *Bombardier*, starring screen veterans Pat O'Brien, Randolph Scott,

Eddie Albert and Robert Ryan, merely *bombs*. Rare shots of early Douglas bombers constitute the picture's only redeeming feature.

Aviation movies in the halcyon days of flying and filmmaking could be as scatterbrained as they pleased, because aviation itself was still largely a hit-or-miss proposition. But aside from some obvious fakery, there were also moments of sheer delight. *Test Pilot*, a 1938 MGM movie filmed at March Field, California, featured previews of the Army's newest big four-engine bomber, the Boeing B-17 Flying Fortress. It also had exciting footage of the Cleveland National Air Races, plus a snappy script that made the most

Stunt pilot Paul Tuntland recreates glider mishap for *Gallant Journey*, the 1946 film biography of John J. Montgomery, who crashed to his death in 1911. Glenn Ford played Montgomery.

of a test pilot's daredevil life and the spectre of death hanging over one flier (Clark Gable), his mechanic (Spencer Tracy), and most of all, his wife (Myrna Loy).

The movie's title is from a book written by the legendary experimental test pilot Jimmy Collins, shortly before he was killed in a crash. One day in 1935 Collins went up to put a new Grumman Navy fighter through its paces. It was to have been his last flight before retiring. Suddenly, in a screaming power dive, a wing sheared off and the whole plane seemed to come apart in the air. Collins had no chance to jump.

In the film, Clark Gable's life as a test pilot is one crack-up after another. One is similar to the crash that killed Jimmy Collins, except in the fictional version the test pilot escapes. (Shots of the plane losing its wings were made with models.) The simulated crash of the Army's new bomber also had its real-life parallel. In 1935 a Boeing 299, the B-17 prototype, fatally cracked up on a test flight because the control locks were not removed. But in the movie Gable survives, while his mechanic, Spencer Tracy, dies.

Although there's as much hard drinking as there is fast flying in *Test Pilot*, the average professional pilot today leads a moderate life. Very few drink in excess, their flying jobs in the modern aeronautical environment are far too demanding. In fact, most of the professional pilots who fly for a living today look and act more like doctors, lawyers or bankers than they do the "intrepid airmen."

Some outstanding footage of barnstorming and air racing also highlights the 1958 Universal release *Tarnished Angels*, an otherwise

Downed fighter pilot (the late William Holden) and would-be rescuer Mickey Rooney run for cover in the 1954 movie *The Bridges at Toko-Ri*, a drama of the Korean conflict based on James Michener's book that questioned the war. (*Frontier* magazine)

On location in San Diego hangar, movie crew prepares to shoot a scene for *Tarnished Angels* (1957), a story of air racing. Robert Stack and Jack Carson lean on wing. (Universal Studios)

mediocre aviation film despite a stellar cast that includes Robert Stack, Rock Hudson, Dorothy Malone and the late Jack Carson. All the flying circus sequences are excellent, but the George Zuckerman screenplay is slow taking off. (Stack is a morbidly taciturn stunt pilot. Hudson, a reporter, falls in love with the pilot's blonde wife, Dorothy Malone.) Finally the big race gets the plot going with everybody at seemingly fever pitch and emotions tugging in opposite directions.

Sadly, most of the movie is difficult to focus in your mind's eye, except for the outstanding cinematography. Stack eventually pays the hero's price, after being an interesting lout on the ground.

That the story is often of secondary importance to what happens in the air couldn't be more apparent than it was in the 1930s. Another good case in point is the James Cagney-Pat O'Brien oldie, *Devil Dogs of the Air,* a Warner Brothers film released in 1935. (Cagney plays the role of the expert stunt pilot and a braggert who joins the Marines because his boyhood hero, O'Brien, is now a Marine officer.) Once again we have a script based on a story by John Monk Saunders, who obviously led the pack in bringing aviation material to the screen.

The picture cost a paltry $350,000 and

took only eight weeks to concoct. Without the full cooperation of the U.S. Navy, however, the production expense would have been greater. The Navy Department threw its entire Marine air fleet into the movie, doing all the flying at naval bases in San Diego and on Long Island. Wrote film critic Beverly Hills: "Embellished with a dedicatory foreword to the iron men of Uncle Sam's army of the sea, this latest red apple to America's warriors is hardly the special production it pretends to be; but for all its carbon-copy story it remains a lively energetic film which is aided considerably by some thrilling air scenes and the pleasant performances of Jimmy Cagney and Pat O'Brien . . . In spite of its story, the film gains a certain interest due to the faultless authenticity of its background, its flying sequences—one of which has Cagney piloting a burning ship—and its understanding of customs and habits of military life and people."

Cagney and O'Brien were also teamed in another Warner Brothers picture the following year, 1936. Called *Ceiling Zero*, the story was adapted from the stage play by Frank Wead. But before the movie's release, commercial airline officials, nervously remembering that many potential air travelers were scared out of their wits during the play's run on Broadway, sent emissaries to plead with the studio. They wanted the production company to withdraw the film.

It was an exercise in futility; the film couldn't be scrapped, there was too much money at stake. However, studio chiefs did allow the airlines to inscribe a foreword to the shadow-drama. "This picture depicts pioneer days in air travel," the caption read. "As a result of these heroic events, we have arrived at today's safety." Naturally, crashes aplenty appeared in the movie. So did the pathetic, bumbling character of a psychopathic pilot who cracked up—and who was now polishing air-port doorknobs and dreaming vaguely of the days when he, too, flew through stormy skies. Needless to say, the airline disclaimer didn't help much.

On the other hand, aviation movies motivated many young men and women to seek careers in aviation during the 1930s. They also attracted flying cadets to the various branches of the armed forces. Paramount's *I Wanted Wings* performed such a service in 1941.

Basically a recruiting film, *I Wanted Wings* was an overlong melodrama with an absurd plot about a murderous golddigger who stows away on a Flying Fortress, Boeing's new B-17 bomber. It starred Ray Milland, William Holden, Brian Donlevy and Wayne Morris, who was destined to become a fighter pilot in his own right in the U.S. Navy. But the film's strongest drawing card was Paramount's newest beauty, Veronica Lake. For this picture, studio publicists billed Veronica as the "Blonde Bomber . . . she flew them into the ground!"

Actually, the movie was promoted as a "thrilling saga of America's flying youth!" Its advertising was beamed at young adventurers: "Ride in a Flying Fortress as it crashes against a mountainside! Dive from a speeding plane—5 miles up—without a parachute! Hedgehop with four 'hot' pilots in the most amazing exhibition of stunt flying every filmed!"

It is fair to say that at the height of World War II every young boy secretly wanted to trade places with the likes of P-38 pilot Van Johnson in the 1943 release of *A Guy Named Joe* as he almost single-handedly cleared the Pacific skies of Japanese Zeroes. Or perhaps the youngster saw himself in the cockpit of a Navy Grumman TBF Avenger torpedo bomber or Douglas SBD Dauntless dive bomber.

The Navy went out of its way to accommodate Hollywood. For example, *Wing and a*

Prayer, made in 1944, was super authentic—mainly because much of the movie was shot aboard the *USS Yorktown II* during her shakedown cruise. At the time, the first Curtiss SB2C Helldivers were attempting to qualify for carrier operation. Their record on the cruise was abysmal; *Yorktown's* commander recommended that the SB2C not be accepted. (The film's title is from the classic line, "He's comin' in on a wing and a prayer," which may have been first used in *Flying Tigers*, John Wayne's 1942 epic costarring Paul Kelly. The words are spoken as Wayne and a baggage handler watch Kelly, with one engine aflame, attempt a fiery landing in a blinding rainstorm.)

While the Navy was most supportive in years past, it obviously would not deliberately wreck operational aircraft for film directors. Thus for crash scenes, 20th Century-Fox solved the problem by salvaging sections of attrited planes and dunking them in huge backlot water tanks. But in *The Malta Story*, a 1954 release by United Artists, reconnaissance pilot Alec Guinness and costar Anthony Steele were photographed standing among the actual remains of RAF Spitfires destroyed in the defense of the Island of Malta during World War II.

The same year—1954—saw Van Johnson appear in another war and another aircraft type as he flew a Grumman F9F Panther in the Korean War movie *Men of the Fighting Lady*, an MGM release. Interestingly, the F9F fuselage mockup used in sound stage process shots

Scene from *Wing and a Prayer* made in 1944 shows Grumman TBF Avenger sinking as gunner Richard Jaeckel struggles out of rear turret while pilot pulls life raft from hatch. (*Frontier* magazine)

In 1944, *Wing and a Prayer* was filmed aboard *USS Yorktown*, even as its new Curtiss SB2C Helldivers underwent service trials. (U.S. Navy)

would be extensively reworked years later to resemble a MiG-21 for MGM's *Ice Station Zebra*.

Three years later—in 1957—Ronald Reagan, the man destined to become our nation's chief executive, appeared in *Hellcats of the Navy* with his second wife, Nancy Davis, whom he met some years earlier as head of the Screen Actors Guild. (It was their only film together.) Interestingly, the now budget-conscious President asserts in his autobiography that the picture could have been better, but studio "string-savers," more concerned about the budget than the script, were the ones who sank *Hellcats*.

Budget considerations, on the other hand, never seemed to bother the legendary Howard Hughes, especially when he wanted to put a good aviation yarn on film. His *Jet Pilot*, also of 1957, starred John Wayne, Janet Leigh, and the U.S. Air Force, and featured some truly breathtaking air-to-air photography. However, the spectacular footage of F-86s, T-33s (playing Russian fighters), and even the Bell-X-1 could not rescue the picture from an implausible plot and some of the silliest dialogue ever put on a soundtrack. The film was withdrawn from distribution shortly after its release and remained "in the can" until after Hughes' death. *Jet Pilot's* first major public appearance didn't come until 1981, when it was shown on NBC-TV.

A popular notion that heroism in aerial warfare represented one of man's most profound expressions of individuality may have peaked around 1958, the year "veteran World

War II fighter pilot" Robert Mitchum roared into "Mig Alley" in 20th Century-Fox's *The Hunters*. Wrote James H. Farmer in the July 1973 issue of *Airpower* magazine:

"In the film wing commander Richard Egan verbally crystallized the idealized image of the steel-nerved, pragmatic American fighter pilot when he noted Mitchum's arrival on the scene in Korea by observing, 'The ice-man cometh.' Mitchum had epitomized that vision of idealized manhood held—consciously or not—by most Americans through the first half of this century. Mitchum was a professional—the best. He didn't say much, because he didn't have to. His actions spoke for themselves. He knew what he wanted and he went after it."

By the early 1960s things began changing for the screen hero. The world had grown smaller, the threat of nuclear destruction was on every American's mind, and people began realizing that acts of one individual can have a very real and personal effect on those about him. "The psychological distance between the audience and the contemporary cinematic hero had narrowed considerably," stated Farmer, "and the birth of the anti-hero was at hand."

Not one to totally concede that the American hero had lost his luster, the late Rod Serling, one of Hollywood's most talented

In the 1953 science fiction thriller *It Came From Outer Space*, Richard Carlson and Barbara Rush use a crop duster's helicopter to search for an alien spaceship in the Arizona desert. (Universal International)

Postwar "baby boom" generation grew up watching *Sky King*. Actors Kirby Grant and Gloria "Penny" Winters, both licensed pilots in real life, were teamed up in the long-running TV series, which featured Cessna T-50 "Bamboo Bomber" and (here) new Cessna 310. (Cessna Aircraft)

The Blue Max (1966) with George Peppard as the brutally ambitious German fighter pilot Bruno Stachel, behind guns here in his Fokker Triplane, explores the "glory" of war. (20th Century-Fox)

writers, turned out a fine screenplay titled *A Time for Glory*. MGM, announcing production in April 1965, billed the film as the first motion picture of the 1960s to "recognize America's new interest in the exploits of World War I's great flying aces." For whatever reason, the picture was never produced.

Robert J. Serling, a former newspaperman and Rod's brother, is also a successful author. His novel *Wings*, published in 1978 by The Dial Press, was optioned for a television mini-series, as was his *She'll Never Get Off The Ground*. *Wings* is an exciting tale of the airline industry. Bob's *The President's Plane Is Missing* was a bestseller in all editions and also became a movie. His *The Left Seat* stands as an aviation classic.

Columbia's *The War Lover* (1961) did much to strip away the once popularly held vision of gallantry and glory in battle. Then, in 1966 20th Century-Fox also revealed the impersonal brutality of modern warfare, but in the context of World War I. Fox's epic *The Blue Max*, in which George Peppard portrays the brutally ambitious German fighter pilot, Bruno Stachel, won acclaim for both its story and cinematography. The flying scenes, filmed on location in Ireland, were among the most spectacular ever created for an aviation-oriented motion picture.

Based on the best-selling novel of the same name by Jack D. Hunter (E. P. Dutton, 1964), *The Blue Max* has no hero unless the hero is man himself who somehow manages eventually to transcend his own degradations. The central character, Bruno Stachel, is the arrogant product of a war-ravaged continent who becomes obsessed with the conviction that he is destined for infallible glory—a god among men.

In the film, Stachel's compulsive desires for prestige and adulation are all embodied in a few sparkling inches of blue enamel and silver, the *Pour le Mérite,* a blue-ribboned cross pendant, Prussia's highest military honor. Nicknamed the "Blue Max" (perhaps in tribute to Max Immelmann, the real life war ace), it was Germany's most important imperial decoration. It has been given to German fighting men for almost two centuries but never before to a flier. (Early in 1916 Oswald Boelcke and Max Immelmann became the first German pilots to receive the Blue Max, after each scored his eighth combat victory. Kaiser Wilhelm himself bestowed the awards. Six months later Immelmann, affectionately known as "The Eagle of Lille," crashed to his death, possibly the result of shooting off his own propeller when his machine gun's synchronizer gear malfunctioned.)

Directed by John Guillermin and produced by Christian Ferry under the supervision of Elmo Williams, head of Fox productions in Europe, the film also starred James Mason, Ursula Andress, Jeremy Kemp and Karl Michael Vogler. Skeets Kelly, who was later killed filming *Zeppelin*, directed second unit photography, which involved all the aerial sequences.

Fox picked Ireland as the production site for several very basic reasons: (1) the terrain was strikingly similar to the Somme areas of France during the latter part of 1918, yet logistically accessible; (2) the surrounding skies were relatively free of other air traffic, smog, fog or air pollution; (3) the Irish Department of Defense offered valuable help; and (4) the green acres of County Wicklow were natural casting; they could be easily churned into a pockmarked battlefield. The big requirement, of course, was the construction of the planes.

Elmo Williams and his associates insisted that the aircraft be authentic reproductions of the original biplanes in which men like Immelmann, Richthofen, Nungesser, Fonck, Rickenbacker and Albert Ball immortalized their

German Pfalz D-III swoops low in strafing attack on Allied troops as British SE-5 bores in from behind. *Blue Max* flying scenes were hailed as some of the best ever filmed. (20th Century-Fox)

names. Nine such World War I fighters were built at a total cost of $250,000, a bargain price by today's standards.

The task was divided among several con-structors and a friendly competition arose to see who could be first in getting their planes built and flown. Douglas Bianchi, an engineer and pilot who tackled one of two Pfalz D-IIIs,

Though reproductions of World War I fighters on both sides were built for The *Blue Max*, producers bolstered fleet by adding Tiger Moths made to look like German aircraft. (20th Century-Fox)

Assault on German airfield routs enemy pilots before they can get airborne; here Bruno Stachel (George Peppard) hurriedly exits his brightly marked Fokker Triplane. (20th Century-Fox)

George Peppard, star of *The Blue Max* and a pilot himself, went through Learjet ground school and actually flew the jet much of the time during nationwide promotion tour. (Gates Learjet)

won the contest, repeating his success building planes under similar conditions for *Those Magnificent Men in Their Flying Machines* a year earlier.

Peter Hillwood, a retired supersonic test pilot, built the other Pfalz, an aircraft type that formed a large part of the German air strength in the first world war. Two British SE-5s were constructed in England by the Miles organization, one time leading makers of light training planes. John Bitz built the two Fokker Dr.1 Triplanes in Germany; Claude Rousseau, three Fokker D-VIIs in France. To make up for his defeat in the construction race, Rousseau proved the airworthiness of his Fokkers by flying one of them to Dublin, Ireland, from Dinard, France, in three hops.

Shortly before he began work on *The Blue Max*, actor George Peppard had learned to fly. While on location in Ireland he flew several of the World War I reproductions, including the Pfalz, an airplane with rather capricious handling characteristics. Peppard also went through a Learjet factory ground school at Wichita, Kansas, so he could log some time at the controls of a high-performance Learjet, which Fox used for a nationwide tour promoting the movie.

In 1968 Paramount acquired *The Blue Max* fleet for *Darling Lili*, described by writer-producer-director Blake Edwards as a "play with music." Released in 1970, the movie stars Edwards' wife Julie Andrews as a British singing idol and secret German spy. The chief target of her World War I espionage is a handsome American squadron commander, played by Rock Hudson, who knows all the crucial Allied military movements.

Fast, sleek Learjets were standard transportation for superspy Derek Flint, played by James Coburn in *Our Man Flint* and *In Like Flint*. (20th Century-Fox)

Hollywood hokum surfaced again in Flint spy spoofs. Here actor James Coburn prepares to leap from a Learjet, actually a full-scale mockup on the studio's backlot (note building under fusealge at lower right). (20th Century-Fox)

Edwards originally named the film *Darling Lili, or Where Were You on the Night You Said You Shot Down Baron von Richthofen?* However, the title was shortened on location in Europe (Dublin, Brussels and Paris) when (but not necessarily because) the budget was "lengthened."

Not even the box office magic of Julie Andrews, who delivered such hits as *Mary Poppins* and *Sound of Music*, combined with the delightful music of Henry Mancini, could make *Darling Lili* a winner. The problem-plagued production seemed to suffer one adversity after another, including long and expensive periods of unsuitable flying weather in Ireland. Despite its top-flight cast, the airplanes and the flying scenes once again stole the show.

The same planes were also used in filming *Richthofen and Brown* and *The Red Baron*. At last report this fine collection of British and German replicas had changed hands several times.

Although fewer pictures with an aerial warfare theme are being made today, filmmakers are still interested in producing high drama adventure movies that involve airplanes and flying. Why?

One reason is the "hype" of the modern flying circus type air show, which is gaining renewed popularity across the country. Like the movies, air shows are entertainment. (The late Sam Goldwyn, a major force in the history of Hollywood, once observed: "The only purpose of a movie is to entertain—if you want to send a message, call Western Union.") Veteran aerobatic performer and motion picture pilot Art Scholl, for example, considers himself first and foremost an *entertainer*.

In fact, the thrilling sport of aerobatic flying is the setting for *Cloud Dancer*, an action-packed Melvin Simon movie released in 1980. While the plot is weak and disjointed, the production contains some of the most dramatic and exciting flying sequences ever seen on film.

Producer-director Barry Brown, himself a pilot and an aeronautical engineer, designed and built a special "Aero Camera" which captured air scenes as never before. Through the magic of Brown's unique camera, the audience can experience the same sights, sensations and visceral thrills as the pilot. The film also features Todd-A0 stereo sound, which is another way of putting the viewer "in the pilot's seat."

David Carradine (playing Brad Randolph) and Joseph Bottoms (Tom Loomis) star in the movie, which involves a world aerobatic championship, a dogfight between a North American P-51 and a Piper Arrow, and a Pitts S-1 barely jumping a car and an 18-wheel truck.

Director Henry Hathaway and actor Stewart Granger discuss scene for *The Last Safari* on location outside Nairobi, Kenya. The 1967 film also starred a Norwegian Learjet. (Paramount Pictures)

Because of their superbly streamlined design, Learjets continue to be favored in any movie or television script calling for a racy-looking, high-performance civil aircraft. (Paramount Pictures)

Carradine, who was not a pilot, had to learn to taxi a Pitts, which is no small feat in itself. He was also flown through a series of punishing precision aerobatic maneuvers in a tandem Pitts S-2A to film his facial expressions and distortions. He endured repeated attacks of airsickness, but "hung in there" through all the aerial shooting without a single complaint.

Professional aerobatic pilots Tom Poberezny, Charlie Hillard and Jimmy Leeward did the key flying. (Tom, an executive with the Experimental Aircraft Association and son of EAA's president, Paul Poberezny, also served as chief pilot and technical advisor.) The two Pitts alone (S-1 and S-2A) flew

over 160 hours for filming.

Crowd scenes were shot at three different air shows in the Phoenix area, location for *Cloud Dancer*. They were filmed in 1978 at Falcon Field, Chandler and Deer Valley airports. Several other noted aerobatic pilots appear as themselves in air show scenes—Gene Soucy, Bill Barber, Leo Loudenslager and Walt Tubb. Tubb, a Western Airlines captain by profession, gets "killed" in the picture flying at one of the storybook air shows. Ironically, Tubb in real life later did crash to his death when he failed to bring his Pitts Special out of a flat spin.

Barry Brown first met Tom Poberezny in

England during the 1972 World Aerobatic Championships. *Cloud Dancer* was Poberezny's first movie, which Brown considered an "important plus" because the flying sequences would not be made in the conventional manner, and Brown wanted a chief pilot who had no preconceived notions about how an aviation film should be made.

Though the movie's plot chases itself in circles for nearly two hours, a good half of the $3.5 million film is devoted to flying—and all flying sequences are for real, filmed from a helicopter or from cameras mounted in or on the aircraft themselves.

Berl Brechner, writing in the May 1980 issue of *Flying* magazine, said this about the film: *"Cloud Dancer* may see moderate suc-

cess. It has touches of violence, illegitimate children, sex, drug-running, drinking and illegal flying—elements that appeal to the crowds filling theaters on the Grade B circuit. Pilots are bound to love it, too—especially if they sleep through all segments except those where airplane engines are running."

Touted as the "first movie on contemporary flying since *Strategic Air Command* in 1955," *Cloud Dancer* gives the general public a good look at sport aviation. And hopefully, it will also serve to create an awareness and appreciation of a new strata of sports hero— the competition aerobatic pilot.

Nothing in *Cloud Dancer*, as in virtually all aviation film, could have been simulated very effectively with models or miniatures.

For *The Last Safari*, this Learjet sported an almost psychedelic zebra stripe. After two weeks in Africa, it was repainted and returned to its owner in Norway. (Paramount Pictures)

Passengers flee plane in *Skyjacked*, MGM's 1972 film depicting an act of air piracy, the crime that brought about strict security measures at every public airport served by scheduled airlines. (Metro-Goldwyn-Mayer)

England's television series titled *Flambards*, a romantic pre-World War I adventure aired in the U.S. over PBS during the summer of 1980, might be an exception. It mixes real flying machines (reproductions of a 1912 Blackburn, Blériot XI, La Demoiselle, two-place Blackburn Mercury and the fictional "Emma" that converts from triplane to monoplane) with radio-controlled flying models. Moreover, in making aviation movies today, highly sophisticated special effects are often blended with the real flying articles.

For example, in one of the most realistic illusions that Hollywood has ever pulled off, a Learjet in the movie *Capricorn One* appears to

strike a car blocking its takeoff, losing its left main landing gear in the process. Even the belly landing that follows is enough to make some movie cynics think that for this particular scene, Warner Brothers actually "wasted" a Learjet. Clay Lacy, who owns the Learjet, did the flying. His longtime friend Don Buchanan handled the copilot duties.

"We did the takeoff scene *thirteen times* to get it right," explained Lacy. "Originally they were going to do a lot of simulation things, but when they saw how close we could come to the cars, the director decided to shoot us instead of a mockup."

"Close" might have been an understate-

195

Art Scholl flies his 1936 Lockheed 12-A for an episode in the TV series *Freebie and the Bean*, in which a "pilot" who has never flown before attempts his first landing on a road. (Art Scholl)

ment, considering the fact Lacy's Learjet cleared the cars by about four feet at 175 miles per hour. During the first take a couple of frightened cameramen leaped from the cartops as Lacy's jet roared toward them. In their scramble to avoid what seemed certain death, they dropped their cameras onto the runway. But other than that, there were no incidents.

Lacy rigged the Learjet so that only one main wheel would raise. As he and Buchanan skim over the parked cars in the scene, the visual impact of clever film editing makes it appear the wheel strikes the windshield. At the same time, a dummy landing gear is fired from the ground. But the audience sees it as it falls. The illusion is perfect.

For the belly landing, the Learjet was flown to California City, eight miles north of Mojave, where the takeoff had been filmed.

There the production crew covered a runway with powdery dirt. When Lucy made a low pass with flaps down, and with cameras positioned at proper angles, the blowing dirt—augmented by a smoke bomb attached to the jet— effectively created the illusion of a high-speed aircraft plowing a furrow across the desert floor.

With more film editing, it looked as though the Learjet had come to rest partially buried in the sand when, in fact, a three-foot deep hole had been dug for the airplane. After rolling the jet into the ditch, the landing gears were wrapped in plastic and the hole filled in with sand. The effect was, indeed, realistic. [*Editor's note:* Another Lacy Learjet— N564CL—was used in an even more incredible stunt when, on a CBS-TV special titled *The Magic of David Copperfield* aired Oct. 26, 1981,

Aerobatic flying is central theme of *Cloud Dancer*, starring David Carradine, in cockpit of Pitts Special. Looking on are director Barry Brown and technical advisor Tom Poberezny. (Melvin Simon Productions)

Dogfight between P-51 Mustang and a Piper Arrow in Arizona mountain passes highlights the action in *Cloud Dancer*, a film filled with thrilling aerobatics. (Melvin Simon Productions)

the aircraft simply vanished from the face of the earth before 50 witnesses and an amazed nationwide audience. Copperfield, 24 years old and 1980's "Magician of the Year," reportedly took eight years to perfect the illusion. Owner Clay Lacy and the author, senior vice president of Gates Learjet, appeared briefly on the show to certify (to guest star Susan Anton) that the Learjet was authentically "stock" and not a magician's prop. "All we've done is drain the fuel," said Lacy, "so this airplane couldn't even move under its own power if it had to." Author Greenwood reports that the illusion set off one

of the largest public reactions in Gates Learjet's history. In one case, an aerospace engineer on the "stealth bomber" project requested to be put in touch with Copperfield; in another, a concerned Gates stockholder demanded to know if the "disappeared" aircraft had been insured or if it would be "written off" out of company profits!]

Lacy, who has been flying for United Air Lines since 1952, operates his own aviation sales and service business, Clay Lacy Aviation, at Van Nuys, California. He flies charter, conducts flight training and performs aerial photography. He also races and holds numerous jet speed records. In 1970 he flew a four-engine Douglas DC-7 airliner with Allen Paulson, now president of Gulfstream American, as copilot in a closed-course pylon race against a bevy of souped-up World War II fighters, finishing sixth in a field of 20. And in 1971 he flew a Learjet 24 to first place in the jet division of the London-Victoria (British Columbia) Air Race.

A past president of the Professional Race Pilots Association, Clay Lacy has flown for over 50 television and theater movies, including *Six Million Dollar Man, Bionic Woman, Mission: Impossible, Airport 75* and *Airport 79.* Among the most recent were *The Inlaws, The Island,* and Clint Eastwood's *Any Which Way You Can,* filmed at Jackson Hole, Wyoming.

In Universal's *The Island,* released in 1980, Lacy's skill as a precision pilot was dramatically demonstrated when he bellied-in a twin-engine Douglas DC-3 exactly on a predetermined spot. The scene called for the DC-3 to crash-land on a small coral airstrip serving the fictitious cay of "Navidad" (actually Marsh Harbor on Great Abaco Island in the Bahamas) in a remote tropical archipelago. Lacy set the big transport down on its retracted wheels, which in a DC-3 extend slightly below the wheel-well fairing when they are in the normal "gear up" mode. As he neared the end of the strip, Lacy kicked the

To create vivid realism in *Cloud Dancer*, actor David Carradine was subjected to punishing G-forces of maneuvers in actual flight. A special camera recorded facial contortions. (Melvin Simon Productions)

Aerial ballet performed for movies by the Red Devils precision flight team—Charlie Hillard, Tom Poberezny, and Gene Soucy. *Cloud Dancer* premiered in May 1980. (Melvin Simon Productions)

Texan Charlie Hillard, a primary pilot on *Cloud Dancer*, won 1972 world precision aerobatic title at the international championship competitions held in France.

Pitts crash in *Cloud Dancer* was simulated by dropping full-scale mockup from a giant crane. This photo caught scene at the instant of impact "during an airshow." (Melvin Simon Productions)

airplane around in a skidding ground loop right in front of the cameras.

The Peter Benchley suspense thriller (Benchley also gave us *Jaws* and *The Deep*) is a gripping tale about a band of latter-day pirates living in an island stronghold who occasionally pick off stray boats to keep their thieving and murdering talents as sharp as their cutlasses. Michael Caine, who plays a journalist trying to find out why more than 600 vessels and 2,000 people have vanished in the region, accidentally stumbles across the buccaneers and becomes a pawn in a deadly game.

Produced by Richard D. Zanuck and David Brown, *The Island* is a gruesome but well-crafted terror/action flick. Lacy's piece of business with the DC-3, incidentally, is the only real flying in the entire picture. But it alone is

worth the price of admission.

In the movie, the DC-3 pilot is a raunchy, slipshod adventurer who puts a 12-year-old boy (Caine's son) in the right seat so airport officials will "think we have two pilots—it's the law." Following the belly landing, the plane blows up. Caine, the boy and the pilot escape the explosion, however. As they look back at the burning wreckage, an island policeman demands a "$20 landing fee," one of the lighter lines in an otherwise heavy and sinister drama.

Another 1980 release, *The Last Flight of Noah's Ark* from Walt Disney Studios, features a spectacular island crash-landing. Based on Ernest K. Gann's story, the plot involves a pilot (Elliott Gould) who agrees to fly a missionary and a load of farm animals to a remote Pacific island in an old B-29. They become lost

For exciting scene in *Capricorn One*, pilot Clay Lacy takes off in Learjet toward cars blocking runway as the "bad guys" in film story race for cover. And what happens next? (Warner Brothers)

and crash-land on another island inhabited only by a pair of Japanese soldiers who haven't heard that World War II is over. The castaways and the Japanese join forces to turn the dam-aged Superfort into a seaworthy *boat* and sail back to civilization. Although the actual crash-landing was cleverly faked, the Confederate Air Force provided a flyable B-29 and the Navy

Learjet stolen by fleeing astronauts appears to strike a parked car, losing its left main landing gear. But scene actually combines flying skill and Hollywood illusion. (Warner Brothers)

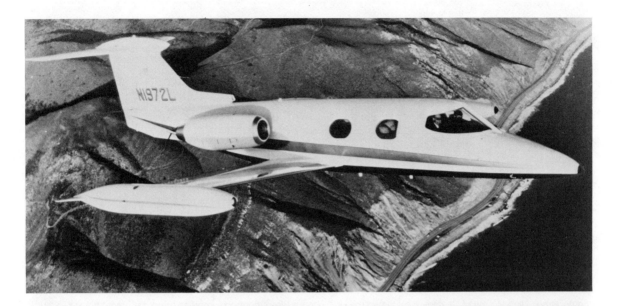

Learjet, top, equipped with Continental Camera Systems' Astrovision, bottom, has made movies of everything from supersonic Concorde to the "Human Fly" who rode atop a DC-8. (Clay Lacy Aviation)

supplied three Superfortress hulks from their China Lake test range for filming; the final result was a believable (if highly unlikely) production. (As improbable as the whole thing sounds, the airplane-to-boat conversion idea isn't all that farfetched. In 1969, a Florida real estate man bought the wingless and engineless remains of a Boeing 307 Stratoliner and con-

Photographer Allen McCoy of Camera West filmed the U.S. Navy's Blue Angels in formation from this Learjet flown by Clay Lacy, a United Airlines captain and movie pilot. (Clay Lacy Aviation)

Clay Lacy, seen here in his famous purple #64 Mustang, once flew a Learjet 17,000 miles with jet-rated UNICEF ambassador Danny Kaye, visiting 65 U.S. and Canadian cities—an all-time record. (Clay Lacy Aviation)

verted the fuselage into a plush, powered houseboat. Interestingly, the Stratoliner—similar to a B-17 with a passenger-carrying fuselage—had previously been owned by two other personalities in this book: Glenn McCarthy, the oil tycoon who lost the $10,000 bet to Paul Mantz, had bought the aircraft—N19904—in 1948 from its original owner, Howard Hughes.)

In the years 1980 and 1981 theatrical and television film production suffered slow-downs, and in some cases abrupt stoppages, because of labor problems. At one time or other during the period, actors, writers and directors walked off the job as their respective guilds sought for them greater benefits, higher pay scales or more equitable finan-cial shares in the lucrative residuals.

Added to Hollywood's difficulties were the steadily increasing expenses associated with filmmaking, costs that were escalating at rates faster than in most other industries. In 1980, for example, according to Frank Rosen-felt of MGM Films, the average production cost per motion picture was $10 million, and the marketing costs $6 million—making the break-even point $16 million. All of which meant, said Rosenfelt, that in order to recoup

A former race pilot, Clay Lacy competed with a finely-tuned P-51. But in 1970 he and Allen Paulson flew this DC-7 transport in a closed-course pylon race. (Clay Lacy Aviation)

For *The Island*, a 1980 release, Clay Lacy executed a perfect belly landing with this DC-3 on a small Bahamian airstrip. To complete the scene, the plane was set on fire. (Clay Lacy Aviation)

such costs, plus the costs of distribution, a new film in 1980 woud have had to gross $40 million or more at the box office before it could show a profit. While as this is written the final numbers are not yet in, suffice to say film production costs in 1981 were relatively higher.

But despite prolonged strikes by essential talent, rising production costs and a dearth of scripts featuring air action, the likes of the Clay Lacys, Jim Gavins and Frank Pines kept reasonably busy with both movie and TV assignments. Even when times are tough, the old established wings of the Hollywood air force somehow manage to launch a few aircraft.

Charlie Hillard, leader of the Eagles aerobatic flight team, served as technical consultant and did most of the flying on the made-for-TV movie *Skyward*, which aired November 20, 1980, over NBC. The show starred the legendary Bette Davis in the role of a former woman stunt pilot who persuades a young female paraplegic (played by newcomer Suzy Gilstrap, in real life a paraplegic) to learn to fly in Bette's Christen Eagle II. Hillard and teammates Gene Soucy and Tom Poberezny fly a trio of Christen Eagles in public exhibitions and for motion pictures and television, including a late 1981 appearance with Art Scholl on ABC-TV's *That's Incredible*. That same ABC show has also featured 60 skydivers linking up in free fall to form a world record human aerial star, and a demonstration of a "disabled" plane landing safely by means of a huge parachute.

The edited version of *Skyward* still ended up with a full 22 minutes devoted to flight scenes, meaning Hillard must have logged a lot of flying in order to get the director's desired footage. Incidentally, *Skyward*'s formal debut took place at the Kennedy Center in Washington, D.C., as part of the ceremonies in which then-President Jimmy Carter proclaimed 1981 as the "Year of the Handicapped."

Miss Gilstrap was such a hit in the original story that she returned to the cockpit in *Skyward Christmas*, carried over the NBC television network on December 3, 1981. As a paraplegic pilot in the holiday sequel, Suzy makes secret plans to fly her grandfather (played by Jack Elam) home for Christmas. The film packs a tremendous emotional and inspirational wallop. It undoubtedly will be repeated. Once again, Charlie Hillard did all the flying.

Two Albert S. Ruddy productions for

Golden Harvest, both of which had arrived in most movie houses by mid-1981, have several thrilling flying scenes. One, *Death Hunt*, is the saga of an obsessed lawman (Lee Marvin) tracking an outlaw trapper (Charles Bronson) through the wilds of the Canadian Northwest. It's the production mentioned earlier, featuring replicas of World War I vintage British Bristol two-place biplane fighters.

The other, *The Cannonball Run*, was directed by veteran stuntman Hal Needham, whose credits also include *Smokey and the Bandit*. The film, a star-studded cross-country auto race, displays one of its best scenes early on, with Burt Reynolds and Dom DeLuise ostensibly at the controls of a Maule M-5 Lunar Rocket (a lightplane famed for its STOL capabilities). DeLuise makes a horrible dis-

covery—they are down to their last can of "refreshment." He gives the tragic news to his partner.

"Let's pull in here and get some beer," says Reynolds, as if he were at the wheel of a Chevy pickup. He proceeds to land the Maule right on the main street of a small town, sending pedestrians and bystanders running for their lives. DeLuise dashes into a convenience store and transacts a purchase of brew. Their supplies restocked, Reynolds roars off down the street again and into the sky.

Air action abounds in PolyGram Pictures' *The Pursuit of D. B. Cooper*, an exciting fictionalized account of a true experience in which a man known only as "D. B. Cooper" parachuted from a hijacked Boeing 727 jetliner, never to be heard from again. The screenplay

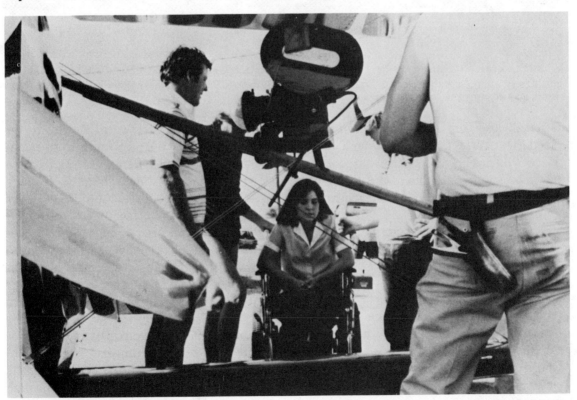

Charlie Hillard, left, was pilot and consultant on *Skyward*, which featured Suzy Gilstrap, shown in wheelchair. Two-hour movie had 22 minutes of flying. (Charlie Hillard)

In NBC's *Skyward*, real-life paraplegic Suzy Gillstrap is taught to fly by Bette Davis, who plays a former aerobatic pilot. The film packs a tremendous emotional and inspirational punch. (Charlie Hillard)

is actually based on the book *Free Fall* by J. D. Reed (Delacorte Press, New York, 1980). Treat Williams plays Cooper, whose fate may never be known, but who is now being commercialized and promoted as a legendary folk hero.

Pursuit was released in November 1981—just 10 years to the month after the real life "Cooper" boarded a Northwest Orient Airlines 727 on Thanksgiving Eve (1971) at Portland, Oregon, and displayed what a flight attendant said looked like dynamite. Demanding four parachutes and $200,000 in $20 bills, Cooper ordered the pilot to fly to Seattle where the plane circled for two and a half hours while authorities gathered the parachutes and money.

At Seattle, the passengers and two of the three flight attendants were allowed to deplane. The money and parachutes were loaded and the jet took off for Reno, Nevada, flying as slowly as possible. Somewhere over southwest Washington State, at an altitude of 10,000 feet, the hijacker, the money and one of the parachutes disappeared through the 727's rear exit door, which had been opened in the air. At this point the film turns to speculation, and the subsequent flying sequences feature perhaps the most impressive crash of a PT-17 Stearman since *Charlie Varrick*.

In real life, only a placard from the inside of the 727's rear stairwell and $5,880 of the money in $20 bills were ever recovered. Cooper's holdup is the nation's only remaining unsolved aerial hijacking for ransom. Since then, 13 persons have tried the same thing, but three were killed and the others were apprehended. [*Editor's note:* As the Federal Aviation Administration's director of public affairs in the early 1970s, author Jim Greenwood was a member of an elite team that manned a special FAA command post while acts of air piracy were in progress. His initimate knowledge of the Cooper crime convinces him that the skyjacker is dead. He also commented that the incident helped revolutionize air travel in the U.S.; it led to more elaborate airport security systems and a redesign of the Boeing 727 jetliner's rear door so that it can't be opened in flight.]

Skydiving sequences in *Pursuit* were directed by Kevin Donnelly, a production manager with MGM who also served as aviation coordinator for the feature movie *Private Ben-jamin* (in which parachutist Mary Wolfrank doubled for actress Goldie Hawn). During the last decade Donnelly and his partner, Ray Cottingham, have filmed scores of parachuting episodes seen in theaters and on TV, including such series as *CHiPS* and *The Six Million Dollar Man*.

Professional parachutists Jerry Meyers, Bill Edwards, Dean Westgaard and Carl Boenish were selected by Donnelly as the basic jumping and filming crew. They represented a highly skilled group of skydivers, averaging about 3,000 jumps each. All were members of SAG—the Screen Actors Guild.

The aerial photographers on *Pursuit* carried both 35 mm movie and 35 mm still cameras. One of them, Carl Boenish, achieved considerable notoriety in November 1981,

Members of the Eagles Aerobatic Flight Team, who are regularly seen flying in theater film and television shows. From left: Gene Soucy, Tom Poberezny and Charlie Hillard, team leader. (Christen Industries)

Flying three Christen Eagle I biplanes powered by 260-hp Lycoming engines with full aerobatic systems and smoke, the Eagles team excels at precision aerobatic flying in close formation. (Christen Industries)

when he and two companions parachuted from the 54-story Crocker Center tower, a newly constructed building 710 feet tall in downtown Los Angeles. Whether or not the jumpers violated any local, state, or federal law appears debatable.

The biggest single expense in staging the scene depicting Cooper bailing out, said Donnelly, was renting a World Airways 727 as a jump platform. It cost $65,000 for two loads of jumpers and cameramen. Clay Lacy's Learjet was also employed for the filming, principally to take shots of the 727 as it traversed the skies before and after Cooper jumped.

The fictionalized pursuit of Cooper races at breakneck speed through several western states, all the way to Mexico. Cooper's nemesis is Bill Gruen (Robert Duvall), an insurance investigator who shrewdly figures out the skyjacker's true identity (J. R. Meade, as in

Reed's novel), because almost no one else could have bailed out of a high-flying jet transport. Gruen knows because he trained "Green Beret" Meade to perform such a feat.

There's a lot of imagination (and some well executed "gags" by stunt coordinator Gary Combs) in the way the chase keeps changing modes, shifting from car to horse to boat (down treacherous white waters) to plane, the latter a somewhat service-worn Stearman cropduster. After Gruen gets hold of the money and drives off, Meade (alias Cooper) grabs the Stearman and resumes the chase. Overtaking Gruen, pilot Meade repeatedly bounces one of his wheels on the car's top as both travel at 90 miles an hour along an open Arizona road, until the inevitable crash of auto and aircraft. Meade and Gruen survive, but split as the film ends.

Art Scholl, doubling for Treat Williams

For *The Pursuit of D.B. Cooper*, a PolyGram picture based on a real skyjacking, pilot Art Scholl flew all the tricky aerial maneuvers, doubling for actor Treat Williams, right, who played the title role. (Deke Houlgate Enterprises)

(D.B. Cooper), pilots the biplane in a demonstration of superb precision flying at extremely low levels. As he plays tag with the speeding car, Scholl must dodge rows of utility lines and some occasional trees, bushes and cacti, all while bumping the auto with his landing gear.

Clay Lacy acted as aviation coordinator for *Red Flag: The Ultimate Game,* a made-for-television movie about the sometimes all too realistic combat fighter training at Nellis Air Force Base, Nevada. The picture, which appeared on the CBS network in the fall of 1981, drew heavily on stock footage from USAF and Northrop film libraries, but shooting certain scenes was still necessary—and expensive. Howard Alston of Marble Arch Productions said the Air Force charged $3,200 an hour for flying each McDonnell F-4, and $1,100 for

Northrop F-5s, which are painted to resemble Russian fighters.

Lacy also directed the aerial sequences for Orion Picture Company's *The Great Santini*, released in late 1980. Marine fighters and fighter pilots were used in filming the movie, which is the story of a career flying officer (Robert Duvall) who tries to make a man out of his sensitive teenage son in the military way. As in *Red Flag,* the aerial scenes in *Santini* are truly spectacular.

Firefox, in which Clint Eastwood has the double role of both producer and star, features a series of special effects that rival *Star Wars*. The actual movements of Clay Lacy's Learjet as it accomplishes the aerial photography are duplicated by computerized model airplanes through an intricate, highly sophisticated electronic recording guidance system. Warner Brothers premiered *Firefox* in the spring of 1982. It's the story of CIA efforts to capture an experimental Russian plane that's far more advanced technologically than anything in U.S. inventories.

The final weeks of 1981 also saw Frank Pine of Tallmantz Aviation working as aviation coordinator on *Winds of War*, a major TV show based on the Herman Wouk book. The story line spans that period in American political and military history between World Wars I and II. Stock footage from *Dive Bomber* and *Tora! Tora! Tora!* supplement new scenes of enemy fighters attacking U.S. installations in the Pacific.

The "fighters" included North American AT-6 and SNJ-2 trainers made over to look like Japanese Zeros. Several of the SNJs are normally seen spewing out advertising smoke as the Skytypers, a skywriting firm. Four other "enemy" aircraft were carefully constructed World War II replicas—one Val, a Kate and two Zekes. The latter previously appeared on *Black Sheep Squadron* and many other World War II movie and television features.

Pilots on the movie came from varied flying backgrounds, their experience ranging from World War II combat to current jet transport flying, air racing, airshow demonstrations and, of course, previous movie work. Among them was Walt Pine, a retired National Guard pilot and brother of Frank Pine, Tallmantz Aviation president.

In CBS-TV's *Red Flag: The Ultimate Game*, a gripping drama about USAF fighter pilot training, Barry Bostwick, left, and William Devane, far right, are fierce competitors. (Marble Arch)

Actor Barry Bostwick climbs into the cockpit of USAF F-4 Phantom in a scene for *Red Flag*, a CBS television production filmed at Nellis Air Force Base, Nevada, in April 1981. (Marble Arch)

Others included Ted Janczarek, airline captain and veteran Hollywood stunt pilot; Glen Riley, an ex-Marine flier; Greg Stinis, owner and operator of Skytypers; Frank Sanders, a skilled airshow exhibition pilot; Jim Maloney of the Planes of Fame Museum, located at Chino Airport; Steve Hinton, accomplished in movie flying and air racing; John Muszala, also associated with the Planes of Fame Museum and an air racer, and Bruce Payne, a pilot with Skytypers who once ferried single-engine lightplanes across the Pacific Ocean.

As air coordinator, Frank Pine was responsible for the scheduled on-camera appearances of the airplanes. But before anyone took to the air, Pine brought his pilots together at the location site and briefed them on camera positions, the designated approaches, the hazardous obstructions in their flight paths, the restricted areas to be avoided and any special requirements for FAA waivers.

Apparently producer/director Dan Curtis chose to focus more on the devastation created by the attacking Japanese aircraft than on the actual flying. As a result, aviation movie buffs may be disappointed in the new scenes. There's lots of dramatic action on the ground, but less of it in the sky, except for some of the clips from other films.

Northrop F-5Es are "Russian" fighters in *Red Flag*. The Air Force program on which the TV movie is based is as close to a "real war" situation as peacetime combat training permits. The Navy's "Top Gun" program is similar. Both services use the F-5 to simulate the size and performance of the Soviet bloc's ubiquitous MiG-21. (Marble Arch)

20th Century-Fox had a number of North American T-6 trainers converted to ersatz Mitsubishi Zeros in the late '60s for *Tora! Tora! Tora!*, and a number have been used regularly in TV and movie work. Here, the "Zeros" hit Wheeler Field for *Tora!* Aero buffs will be glad to know that the exploding P-40s are just fiberglass and tube steel replicas made for the movie; Frank Tallman's P-40E was used as the master for the fiberglass molds. (20th Century-Fox)

Winds of War stars Robert Mitchum as the leading figure in a cast of hundreds. Other principal players include Ali MacGraw, Ralph Bellamy, Ben Murphy, Polly Bergen, John Houseman, Peter Graves, Jan-Michael Vincent, Scott Brady and Victor Tennant, to name a few. It is a long production—16 hours in all. At this writing the film is scheduled for telecasting in two three-hour and five two-hour parts in February 1983. A sequel, *War in Remembrance*, may also be in the offing.

Ever since the first action films of some 70 years ago, death has stalked the ranks of motion picture production personnel in their pursuit of excellence—a small strip of film that may stand out as a masterpiece of high drama, coupled with artistic splendor and award-winning cinematography. But in less than a year's time recently three assistant cameramen were killed while filming stunts, including Jack Tandberg, who was hit by a car that went off course during the shooting of a television movie.

As it so often follows, this latest rash of fatal accidents spurred a number of new safety measures in the motion picture and television industries. Stated a bold advertisement in an April 1981 edition of a prominent entertainment trade publication: "There is no shot worth a life."

Ironically, one of Hollywood's worst tragedies of recent times didn't happen behind

Lineup of stock and modified T-6 and SNJ-2 trainers used as Japanese and American combat aircraft in *Winds of War*. The Pearl Harbor attack was recreated and filmed at Point Magu Naval Base on December 7, 1981, the 40th anniversary of the real event. (Skytypers via Greg Stinis)

A "Texan" becomes a "Zeke" as U.S. star is overpainted with Japanese *hinomaru* during break in *Winds of War* filming. Skytypers, a skywriting company of Los Alamitos, Cal., provided six SNJ-2s for the picture. (Skytypers via Greg Stinis)

or even in front of the camera. On May 22, 1981, at Timberline Lodge on Mount Hood, Oregon, noted film director Boris Sagal, 58, had just finished a third day of shooting for the NBC-TV movie *World War III*, which is about a Russian attack on the Alaskan oil pipeline. (It stars Rock Hudson and David Soul.) Most of the director's work had been for television; his credits include *The Oregon Trail, The Dream Makers* and *Ike*.

Up until that day in Oregon, Sagal's best known theatrical film involving flying was probably *The Thousand Plane Raid*. And in all the years since he first began directing films back in 1963, the popular and talented director frequently worked in and around aircraft of all types—and often under rather hazardous conditions. Yet on this particular day, a helicopter

used for filming *World War III* dropped down out of the sky and landed on a Timberline Lodge parking lot, where some of the production crew awaited. Before anyone could stop him, Sagal walked toward the rear of the machine, and suddenly turned into the spinning tail blades. He died at a Portland hospital five hours later.

As hard as movie flying is on the people involved, however, it's even harder on the aircraft. This is particularly regrettable when the airplanes are rare and historic craft, such as the Mosquito burned in *633 Squadron* or the B-25 set ablaze for *Catch-22*. The carnage continues, much to the chagrin of airplane lovers; the DC-3 so skillfully crashed by Clay Lacy for *The Island* was not blown up by harmless special effects, but "for real"—the destruction of

Helicopter carrier *USS Peleliu* played part of WWII-era carrier for *Winds of War*. *Peleliu's* deck was too short for fixed-wing landing, so SNJ-2 was craned aboard. (Skytypers via Greg Stinis)

Greg Stinis, president of Skytypers, and SNJ-2 aboard *Peleliu*. Aircraft was painted to represent Douglas SBD Dauntless dive bomber in pre-WWII paint scheme. (Skytypers via Greg Stinis)

Winds of War birds over Long Beach, California. *Queen Mary II* and dome housing Howard Hughes' "Spruce Goose" are visible just off nose of the "Zero." (Skytypers via Greg Stinis)

the old bird was total and absolute. According to Lacy, nothing was salvageable. Nor could the scene have been retaken without securing another expendable DC-3. Yet even as smoke poured from the fiery Douglas carcass and the episode came to its desired conclusion, the happiest man in the production company was undoubtedly director Michael Ritchie, for he knew he had on film precisely what he wanted.

Very likely a pleased second unit director on location, turning to his crew of technicians and cameramen, called out those few simple but heartening words that—in typical Hollywood tradition—signaled the end of a successful shooting . . .

"Okay, people—it's a wrap!"

Epilogue

Motion pictures have come a long way since the turn of the century—technologically and artistically. So has flying. And the advances of both have been at a fantastic pace. Together, men, machines, and cameras have flown to the moon and back. Unfortunately, too many of us still take for granted the marvels and miracles we have achieved.

That is, unless we've been to the Smithsonian Institution's National Air and Space Museum in Washington, D.C. In the five years after its grand opening in 1976, America's bicentennial anniversary year, more than 50 million people visited the museum, an international record. It is not an exaggeration to say that everyone old enough to comprehend comes away with a renewed sense of awe and shared pride in our incredible accomplishments.

Nowhere else in the world has been assembled such massive proof that some of our most primal dreams can and do come true. A tour through NASM is a voyage of discovery—and movies play a role as vital in the storytelling of flight as the superbly sophisticated and highly dramatic exhibit techniques themselves.

Perhaps one reason NASM has become the biggest tourist attraction in Washington is because so much of the collection represents specific events the average person can recall, or at least relate to.

When a visitor moves among the exhibits, he is not just looking at a gathering of objects, he is reliving an experience, whether it be the first time he took a commercial airline flight, served in a war, flew his own airplane, cheered Lindbergh's flight over the Atlantic or Apollo 11's communications from the moon. At one time or another, a major portion of the museum's exhibits made world headlines.

Close to 100 different motion pictures showing aircraft in actual combat, being flight tested, breaking records or crashing, supplement and complement the splendid array of artifacts that document our aeronautical progress.

There is also *To Fly,* NASM's first spectacular film salute to America. It is shown daily in the museum's IMAX theater on a movie screen five stories high and seven stories wide. This film, produced by Academy Award winner Francis Thompson, quite literally overwhelms each visitor who watches it. Photographed in 70mm film (a frame dimension double the size of a standard theater frame, virtually eliminating "grain"), *To Fly* is a breathtaking 30-minute cinematic ex-

Shrine of flight: The National Air and Space Museum of the Smithsonian Institution in Washington, D.C., houses the inspiring story of flight from early balloons to spacecraft. (Smithsonian NASM)

perience that takes its audience on a bird's-eye tour of the nation from 1831 to the year 2002.

Because of the immense size of the screen and the theater's steeply sloping auditorium seating, viewers have a sense of motion. And they actually "feel" part of it all. Many, in fact, can be seen clinging white-knuckled to the armrests of their chairs as a biplane flips upside down or the Navy's crack Blue Angels precision aerobatic team screams across the Arizona desert. "Airsickness" is not unknown.

For Greg MacGillivray and James Freeman, who co-directed and co-photographed the movie, all the aerial scenes were difficult, but if something had gone wrong, they could have been retaken. The most critical shot of the entire film was one photographed from the ground—the liftoff of the towering Saturn rocket that boosted the Apollo as-

tronauts into orbit in 1975 for their linkup with the Soviet Soyuz spacecraft during the Apollo-Soyuz Test Project. It just happened to be the last Saturn launched.

Also produced by Francis Thompson, the museum's second feature film, equally as spectacular as *To Fly,* is titled *Living Planet.* Here viewers are carried on an aerial journey over many of the Earth's remote places—Africa, India and the Arctic.

But a third 70mm movie made for the NASM theater will have a special appeal to aviation buffs. It's a half-hour drama titled *Flyer,* the first fully theatrical, fictional story filmed in the IMAX format. It has everything for the airman—action, adventure, daring feats of flying. It's a warm and visually exciting story of people who share a love of flight.

Flyer, produced by MacGillivray/ Freeman Films and Dennis Earl Moore Pro-

Space Hall in Smithsonian's NASM features everything from mighty rockets to Skylab orbital workshop. More than 10,000,000 persons of all ages visit the museum each year. (Smithsonian NASM)

A Place of Dreams, a 1979 PBS special, is fitting description of NASM. Seen here are Lindbergh's *Spirit of St. Louis*, 1903 Wright Flyer, and John Glenn's *Friendship 7*. (Smithsonian NASM)

ductions, and sponsored as a public service by Conoco, features the flying exploits of a stunt pilot and World War II veteran and his eager young protege. Aircraft of all types figure in the action, from sailplanes and helicopters to vintage biplanes and a restored F4U Corsair.

Art Scholl served as air coordinator and primary pilot. Other fixed-wing pilots were Chuck Wentworth, Bob Aumack, Jim Osborne, and Brian and Bernie Goodlove. Helicopter pilots included Karl Wickman, Ross Reynolds, Rick Holly and Harry Haus. Stuntman on the film was Kevin Donnelly, who specializes in thrilling parachute sequences.

The central character, "Kyle Murphy," is a devoted restorer of old aircraft and premiere

Rockwell International executive Bob Hoover, a former North American test pilot, flies his P-51 through an aerobatic routine as spectacular as anything ever done in an airplane. Film featuring Hoover's famous trademark "Tennessee Walk" landing in the Mustang runs continuously at National Air and Space Museum's gallery of exhibition flight. (Rockwell International)

Hollywood stunt pilot. He is a mentor and hero to "Tim," the young son of a wartime flying buddy. Scenes of Navy carrier operations, motion picture stunting and precision aerobatic flying are among the breathtaking elements that make this newest big screen film a memorable viewing experience.

But ever more meaningful to nostalgic aviation movie fans, the montage of flying scenes in *Flyer* embodies the spirit and love of flight that motivated men like Frank Tallman, Paul Mantz and Dick Grace.

The way thousands of people of all ages flock to NASM every week suggests that a resurgence of national interest in movies about airplanes and flying is in the offing. Well, it hasn't happened yet. Few aviation films are being made today, for either theater or television. The main reason is economics. Many studios cannot afford to gamble millions on a flying color spectacular.

However, in recent years some of these same studios have invested heavily in a number of science fiction movies that require

Scene from *To Fly*, NASM's spectacular salute to the wonders of flight. Photographed on 70mm film, the movie projects on a special IMAX screen five stories high. (Smithsonian NASM)

enormously expensive special effects. Certainly that's to the good. Obviously, it's what the public wants.

It all started a dozen years ago with Stanley Kubrick's magnificent *2001: A Space Odyssey*, which raised the "sci-fi" film from the quickie serial and cheapie action flick to a glorious and expensive spectacle. Now the screen craze is outer space wars. No movie in

Hollywood history, in fact, has matched the combined artistic and commercial triumph of George Lucas' 1977 epic, *Star Wars*. Its sequel, *The Empire Strikes Back*, also established some new box office records.

These and other science fiction movies like *Star Trek, The Black Hole, Close Encounters of the Third Kind* and *Alien*, along with the TV series *Battlestar Galactica* (ABC) and

NBC's *Buck Rogers in the 25th Century,* have opened a new *genre* in creative cinematography. Whether the story revolves around grotesque enemy invaders from another planet or a monstrous enigma so powerful that it swallows stars and whole solar systems, the new adventure thrillers (made with elaborate models and miniatures) have brought back the good guys in white and the bad guys in black.

What's really encouraging is that even the anti-establishment forces seem to see nothing wrong with the idea of films depicting war in outer space—or projects involving billions for the further exploration of our universe.

Most of these movies, of course, are masterpieces of deception. While the graphic illusions are generally excellent, individual films often contain gross technical errors, such as the one in the now defunct television series *Battlestar Galactica.* (In it, men and women parachute out of a spacecraft with no spacesuits and the parachutes open in outer space—where there is no atmosphere.) If nothing else, such fantasies may serve as an inspiration for a coming generation of scientists.

George Lucas sees a steadily growing science fiction movie market through the year 2001. Apparently so does the American Film Institute (AFI). Early in 1980 the AFI initiated a special educational course for youngsters called *Out of This World Sci Fi Movie Making.*

The need to educate the public on the benefits of probing space ("without information, there's no knowledge") was undoubtedly John Denver's motivation when he presented his television special *The Higher We Fly* over

To Fly engulfs and overwhelms its audience in dizzy panorama that puts across an exuberant illusion of being truly airborne. It is a high tribute to aviation filmmaking. (Smithsonian NASM)

Size of film and screen, 50 feet high and 70 feet wide, enabled *To Fly* producers to play on viewer's sensations. Watching 30-minute movie can be almost as much fun as flying. (Smithsonian NASM)

Silhouetted against the setting sun, a modern hang glider challenges drafts against Pacific cliffs, silently playing with winds and currents and enjoying true freedom of flight. (Smithsonian NASM)

the ABC network in June 1980. While the show examined the history of flight from early ballooning to the space shuttle, Denver's message came through loud and clear: We should *look up* to the future.

Millions of fans around the world know him as a singer and actor, but there's also John Denver the pilot. Taught to fly by his father, Henry "Dutch" Deutschendorf, a retired Air Force colonel, the genial entertainer often takes command of his Learjet during cross-country trips.

After looping the loop in a barnstormer's biplane, viewers roar low over the wide expanse of Arizona with Navy's Blue Angels, then take an eagle's eye cruise above Manhattan. (Smithsonian NASM)

Denver also enjoys swooping over his beloved Rocky Mountains in the cockpit of a Skybolt, an experimental biplane that he piloted in his TV special. In the show he also flew: (1) a hot air balloon over Snowmass, Colorado, (2) a reproduction of the original 1903 Wright brothers' Kitty Hawk Flyer, (3) a supersonic USAF F-15 Eagle, and (4) the

Movie frame from *To Fly* shows Saturn launch for 1975 Apollo-Soyuz Test Project. America's space probes have made many important contributions to the quality of life on Earth. (Smithsonian NASM).

Stuntman Kevin Donnelly and pilot Art Scholl, following a scene for *Flyer*. Note the 70mm IMAX camera mounted on left wing of the Stearman. That's a dummy camera between the cockpits. (Dennis Earl Moore)

To show a movie in the making, crew in "cherry picker" bucket at left has camera trained on "shooting tower" at lower right, where "cameramen" in *Flyer* are "filming" a World War I sequence. (Dennis Earl Moore)

232

Hollywood magic is used to create dogfight between onrushing Fokker Triplane and a Nieuport 28, the latter rigidly fixed to an angled platform in foreground. Scene appears in *Flyer*. (Dennis Earl Moore)

Technicians on *Flyer*, a big screen production for the National Air and Space Museum, prepare a Nieuport 28 for simulated air action. IMAX camera at right will film scene from behind tail. (Dennis Earl Moore)

In *Flyer* finale, Tim (actor Perry Lang) rolls Blanik L-13 behind Kyle Murphy (Roy Cooper) in Schwiezer, with nose-mounted IMAX camera. Real pilots were Art Scholl and Chuck Wentworth. (Dennis Earl Moore)

space shuttle simulator in the Johnson Space Center at Houston—a mock flight in which he took the viewer from re-entry to touchdown, a sequence intercut with actual footage of the shuttle in operation.

All of this was to demonstrate how far we have come in less than 80 years. Denver then discussed with astronomer Jesse Greenstein of the Mount Palomar Observatory the question of what man will find when he ventures into deep space. ("There is no end to the universe; there are doors beyond doors.") Finally he urged his fellow Americans to consider the

vast technological developments of recent years and direct themselves to new frontiers. (It is noteworthy that for *The Higher We Fly* Denver and his production associates in April 1981 received the prestigious Earl D. Osborn Award sponsored by the EDO Corporation, makers of aircraft components, accessories and instruments. The award is the highest honor given by the Aviation/Space Writers Association in the general aviation category.)

A planned NBC series titled *Escape Velocity* documents the inspiring story of the U.S. space program—from America's 1957 embar-

For close-ups of Fokker Triplane burning, *Flyer* technicians rig plane to rocker platform, which simulates flight motion. Wind machine can barely be seen behind light reflectors. (Dennis Earl Moore)

Man's outreach in space has also given us new knowledge of Mars, Venus, Jupiter, and Saturn. But it is only the beginning. As John Denver would say, "We must look up to the future." (Smithsonian NASM)

rassment when the Russians launched their Sputnik satellite, to Neil Armstrong's walk on the moon. Much of the show will use actual NASA footage. "It's some of the most dramatic film you'll ever see," says co-producer Mike Gray.

The Higher We Fly brought back memories of the early pioneers, the battle aces, the barnstormers and the great air races. It also recalled a rich heritage that has not been lost, a heritage preserved in the hundreds of movies of classic machines flown by courageous pilots—the Locklears, the Wilsons, the Clarkes, the Turners, the Graces, the Mantzs, the Rankins, the Tallmans and the rest. Theirs is a legacy that will long endure.

The many air epics made possible by a cadre of pioneering Hollywood fliers and their disciples represented the hopes and dreams of a far simpler world. Because of them—and all the others who have "slipped the surly bonds of earth"—we can clearly see the wonder of the future mirrored in the glory of the past . . .

Think about it.

Bibliography

Andrist, Ralph K., and the editors of American Heritage. *The American Heritage History of the 20's & 30's*. New York: American Heritage Publishing Co., Inc., 1970.

Ault, Phil. *By the Seat of Their Pants*. New York: Dodd, Mead & Company, 1978.

Benchley, Peter. *The Island*. Garden City, New York: Doubleday and Company, Inc., 1979.

Blanchard, Nina. *How to Break into Motion Pictures, Television, Commercials & Modeling*. Garden City, New York: Doubleday & Company, Inc., 1978.

Brownlow, Kevin. *Hollywood: The Pioneers*. New York: Alfred A. Knopf, Inc., 1979.

Burke, John. *Winged Legend, The Life of Amelia Earhart*. New York: G.P. Putnam's Sons, 1970.

Caidin, Martin. *Barnstorming*, New York: Duell Sloan and Pearce, 1965.

———. *Everything But the Flak*. New York: Duell, Sloan and Pearce, 1964.

———. *The Saga of Iron Annie*. Garden City, New York: Doubleday & Company, Inc., 1979.

Catto, Max. *Murphy's War*. New York: Dell Publishing Co., Inc., 1968.

Cleveland, Carl M. *"Upside-Down" Pangborn*. Glendale, California: Aviation Book Company, 1978.

Collins, Jimmy. *Test Pilot*. New York: The Sun Dial Press, 1935.

Davidson, George E. *Beehives of Invention, Edison and His Laboratories*. National Park Service, U.S. Department of the Interior, Washington, D.C., 1973.

Dietrich, Noah, and Thomas, Bob. *Howard, The Amazing Mr. Hughes*. Greenwich, Connecticut: Fawcett Publications, Inc., 1972.

Dwiggins, Don. *The Air Devils*. Philadelphia and New York: J.B. Lippincott Company, 1966.

———. *Hollywood Pilot, The Biography of Paul Mantz*. Garden City, New York: Doubleday & Company, Inc., 1967.

Gann, Ernest K. *A Hostage to Fortune*. New York: Alfred A. Knopf, 1978.

———. *Flying Circus*. New York: Macmillan Publishing Co., Inc., 1974.

Goldman, William, and Hill, George Roy. *The Great Waldo Pepper*. New York: Dell Publishing Co., Inc., 1975.

Goodman, Ezra. *The Fifty-Year Decline and Fall of Hollywood*. New York: Simon and Schuster, Inc., 1961.

Grace, Dick. *Visibility Unlimited*. New York: Longmans, Green and Co., 1950.

———. *Squadron of Death*. Garden City, New York: The Sun Dial Press, Inc., 1937

Griffith, Richard, and Mayer, Arthur. *The Movies*. New York: Simon and Schuster, 1957, 1970.

Higham, Charles. *Cecil B. DeMille*. New York: Charles Scribner's Sons, 1973.

Lasky, Jesse L., Jr. *Whatever Happened to Hollywood*. New York: Funk & Wagnalls, 1975.

Mikesh, Robert C. *Excalibur III: The Story of a P-51 Mustang*. Washington, D.C.: Smithsonian Institution Press, 1978.

Parke, Robert B., and the editors of *Flying. The Best of Flying*. New York: Van Nostrand Reinhold Company, 1977.

Ronnie, Art. *Locklear: The Man Who Walked On Wings*. New York: A.S. Barnes and Company, 1973.

Sadoul, Georges. *Dictionary of Film Makers*. Los Angeles: University of California Press, 1972.

Saunders, John Monk. *Wings*. New York: Grosset & Dunlap by arrangement with G.P. Putnam's Sons, 1927.

Scheuer, Steven H. *The Movie Book*. Chicago: The Ridge Press and Playboy Press, 1974.

Schickel, Richard. *The Men Who Made the Movies*. New York: Atheneum, 1975.

Skogsberg, Bertil. *Wings On The Screen* (English language edition). San Diego, California: A.S. Barnes & Company, Inc., 1981.

Tallman, Frank. *Flying the Old Planes*. Garden City, New York: Doubleday and Company, Inc., 1973.

Thompson, Scott. "Hollywood Mitchells: The Story of the Tallmantz B-25 Bombers," *Air Classics*. Canoga Park, California: Challenge Publications, Inc., September, 1980.

Wellman, William A. *A Short Time for Insanity*. New York: Hawthorn Books, Inc., 1974.

Wolf, Marv. "Making War Movies" Part I, *Soldier of Fortune*. Boulder, Colorado: Omega Group Ltd., July, 1981.

Zukor, Adolph, with Kramer, Dale. *The Public Is Never Wrong*. New York: G.P. Putnam's Sons, 1953.

Index

243

Edited by Steven Mesner